The English Radical Tradition
1763-1914

EDITED BY

S. MacCoby, M.A., Ph.D.

GREENWOOD PRESS, PUBLISHERS
WESTPORT, CONNECTICUT

Library of Congress Cataloging in Publication Data

Maccoby, Simon, ed.
    The English radical tradition, 1763-1914.

    Reprint of the ed. published by New York University
Press, New York.
    Includes index.
    1. Great Britain--Politics and government.
2. Great Britain--Social conditions. I. Title.
[DA472.M3 1978]   320.5'0941   78-681
ISBN 0-313-20284-2

First published in 1952

Reprinted with the permission of New York University Press

Reprinted in 1978 by Greenwood Press, Inc.
51 Riverside Avenue, Westport, CT. 06880

Printed in the United States of America

10 9 8 7 6 5 4 3 2 1

GENERAL PREFACE

ONE of the unique contributions the English people have made to civilisation has been the discussion of political issues which has been going on in Britain continuously since the sixteenth century. It is a discussion which has ranged over the whole field of political thought and experience. It began with the relation of the State to the individual in religious matters; for the last half century it has been increasingly preoccupied with the relation of the State to the individual in economic matters. The strength of tradition, the right of rebellion; the demand for equality, the rights of property; the place of justice and morality in foreign policy, the relations between Britain and her overseas territories; the claims of minorities, the value of civil and religious freedom; the rule of law, the Rule of the Saints; the rights of the individual, the claims of the State—all these have been the subject of passionate and incessant argument among Englishmen since the time of the Reformation.

This debate has never been of an academic character. There are, it is true, masterpieces of political philosophy in the English language: Hobbes' *Leviathan* is an obvious example. But the true character of this debate has been empirical: the discussion of particular and practical issues, in the course of which a clash of principle and attitude is brought out, but in which the element of abstract thought is always kept in relation to an immediate and actual situation. The riches of British political thought are to be found less in the philosophers' discussions of terms like 'The State', 'freedom' and 'obligation'—important though these are—than in the writings and speeches on contemporary political issues of men like Lilburne, Locke, Bolingbroke, Burke, Tom Paine, Fox, the Mills, Cobden, Disraeli, Gladstone, and the Fabians. No other literature in the world is so rich in political pamphlets as English, and the pages of *Hansard* are a mine not only for the historian of political events but also for the historian of political ideas. It is in the discussions provoked by the major crises in British history—the Civil War, the Revolt of the American Colonies, the Reform Bills of the nineteenth century—that our political ideas have been hammered out.

One unfortunate result of this is that much of the material which anyone interested in English political ideas needs to read is inaccessible. Pamphlets and speeches are often only to be found in contemporary publications hidden away on the more obscure shelves of the big libraries. Even when the reader has secured a volume of seventeenth-century pamphlets or of Gladstone's speeches, he may well be deterred by the large amount of now irrelevant detail or polemic through which he has to make his way before striking the characteristic ideas and assumptions of the writer or speaker. It is to meet the need of the reader who is interested in English political ideas but has neither the time, the patience, nor perhaps the opportunity, to read through a library of books to find the material he is looking for that this present series of books is designed. Its aim is to present from sources of the most varied kind, books, pamphlets, speeches, letters, newspapers, a

selection of original material illustrating the different
facets of Englishmen's discussion of politics. Each
volume will include an introductory essay by the editor
together with sufficient explanation of the circumstances to make each extract intelligible. In some cases
it has seemed best to make a particular crisis the focus
of the discussion: this has been done with Mr. Beloff's
volume, *The Debate on the American Revolution,*
and with Dr. Cobban's *The Debate on the French
Revolution.* In other cases the development of a
particular view has been traced over a long period of
years: this is the case, for instance, with the volumes on
the Conservative, the Liberal, and the Radical Traditions. In a third case, that of the volume on *Britain
and Europe,* our idea has been to single out a recurrent
problem in English politics and trace its discussion from
Pitt's day to our own.

To begin with, we have concentrated our attention
on the period between the Revolt of the American
Colonies and the Great War of 1914. When that has
been covered we hope to treat the earlier period in the
same way, notably the political discussions of the
seventeenth century.

We do not believe that any one of these facets can
be singled out and labelled as in some particular way
more characteristic than others of the British Political
Tradition: the rebels have as great a part in our political tradition as those who have argued the case for the
claims of prescription and established authority. The
wealth of that tradition is that it includes Lilburne,
Tom Paine, Richard Cobden and the Early English
Socialists as well as Locke, Burke and Disraeli.

We have tried to hold the balance even. In no sense
do we wish to act as propagandists or advocates. While

each editor has been given complete freedom to present his material as he wishes, we have been concerned as general editors to see that equal representation is given to different views in the series as a whole. Only in this way, we believe, is it possible to display the British Political Tradition in its unequalled richness, as built up out of a variety of political opinions and out of the clash between them, as the great and continuous debate of the nation to which, in its very nature, there can be no end.

ALAN BULLOCK

F. W. DEAKIN

Oxford

TABLE OF CONTENTS

TABLE OF CONTENTS

xi

TABLE OF CONTENTS

INTRODUCTION

It was during the struggle against George III's increasing domination of politics and Parliament, between 1762 and 1782, that modern British Radicalism was born. The famous phrases, " rotten boroughs " and " King's Friends ", were among the earliest coinages of Opposition politicians, suspicious of the King's methods and ultimate intentions, and there were, besides, older agitations to draw on for invective against " bribery and corruption ", " placemen and pensioners ", the Civil List and the Septennial Act. George III's ability, however, in 1769, to rally great Parliamentary majorities against Wilkes and the Wilkes mobs, and against what were deemed the rights of the electorate, produced a further development. The City of London, much under the influence of the wealthy Alderman Beckford, led a nation-wide campaign of protest and demonstration which lasted for years. Early in its course, Beckford was made Lord Mayor and, with Horne Tooke at his elbow, produced the most strongly-worded City Petitions ever presented at Court during the eighteenth century.

Why the City Petition, presented at St. James's on March 14, 1770, deserves mention in any account of Radical origins, can be made plain by a short quotation. The attack on George's Ministers and their Parliamentary majority ended with these words[1]:

Since, therefore, the misdeeds of your Majesty's ministers in violating the freedom of election, and depraving the noble con-

[1] *Annual Register*, 1770, Appendix to the Chronicle, p. 201.

I

stitution of Parliaments, are notorious . . . and since your Majesty, both in honour and justice, is obliged inviolably to preserve them, according to the oath made to God and your subjects at the coronation, We, your Majesty's remonstrants, assure ourselves, that your Majesty will restore the constitutional government and quiet of your people, by dissolving this Parliament, and removing those evil ministers for ever from your councils.

The protest demonstrations of 1769 and 1770 were not, however, the only paths along which Beckford, with Horne Tooke and Wilkes as his guides and with Chatham leading a large part of the Parliamentary Opposition in applause, sought to take the City and the country. In the famous meeting of City Freemen of March 6, which adopted the Petition and Remonstrance to the King quoted above, Beckford gave the Freemen a *Political Creed*, of which the gist, according to the prints of the time, was no less than the following[1]:

That the number of little paltry rotten boroughs, the number of placemen and pensioners, and the corruption of the electors as well as the elected, were the instruments that would in time prove the ruin of the state. To prevent those evils it was necessary that there should be a more equal representation of the people, that the number of placemen should be limited by law, and that the servants of the crown should be obliged to exhibit fuller accounts of the manner in which the public money was disposed of.

The phrase "more equal representation of the people" opened a special chapter of its own in constitutional history.

Beckford died in June 1770, but his campaign against the King and the Court had the effect of handing over the City's local government to forces which used it for years to stage demonstrations against George III's

[1] *Gentleman's Magazine*, March 1770, p. 109.

Ministers and their majority. The annals of the period between 1770 and 1782 are full of the exploits which such "patriots" as Brass Crosby, Oliver, Sawbridge, Townshend, and Watkin Lewes were able to undertake as City Aldermen, Sheriffs, Mayors or Members of Parliament, although, as might be expected, Wilkes outdid them all in ability to make trouble for the King and his Government whether as Alderman Wilkes, Mr. Sheriff Wilkes or Lord Mayor. It was as M.P. for Middlesex, that on March 21, 1776, in the House of Commons, Wilkes opened the Parliamentary history of Reform by his motion, "That leave be given to bring in a Bill, for a just and equal representation of the people in Parliament". Extracts from the speech he made on that occasion are given in Document 5, and they show how fully the whole history of "rotten boroughs" had now been investigated, and on what grounds Wilkes was prepared to ask for the enfranchisement even of the labouring poor.

The agitators for change made a further step forward when they captured and applied to their own purposes a word so full of attraction to many solid elements in the country as "reformation". Cartwright, for instance, was using the word in 1777 in talking of "a thorough and compleat parliamentary reformation", and was advocating "annual parliaments" and "equal representation" as the "radical cure" for parliamentary corruption. Cartwright and many others had, by 1777, acquired the conviction that the Crown and Ministry had completely mishandled the American question and that a corrupt Parliament, instead of acting as a check, had served as a tool. When further dangers appeared after the intervention of France, on the American side, in 1778 and of Spain in 1779, and when, in addition, the dislocation of trade and war-taxation threatened to become intolerable, some of the most conservative elements in the country did not hesitate to join the agitators in calling for " Public Oeconomy ". This it was hoped to secure by such measures as the disqualification of Government contractors from membership of Parliament, the disqualification of Customs and Excise officers from voting at elections, the severe limitation of the Pension List and the abolition of a large number of sinecure posts at Court and in the Government Departments.

Though not averse to advocating all possible ways of striking " a good stout blow at the influence of the Crown ", those pressing for a radical parliamentary reformation found, in the conditions of 1780, a special chance of urging Universal Suffrage and Annual Parliaments. In fact, the Report of their Sub-Committee at Westminster (printed below as No. 7) demanded also Vote by Ballot, Equal Electoral Constituencies, Payment of Members, and Abolition of the Property Qualification. On June 2, 1780, the Duke of Richmond, speaking in the House of Lords, moved the first reading of a Bill for Annual Parliaments and Universal Suffrage. But it was during his very speech that the destructive rioting of the Gordon " Protestant " mobs began, riots which were to provide one of the strongest arguments against radical reform for decades. Certainly, the Rockingham Cabinet, of which Richmond himself became a member, while undertaking to disfranchise Customs and Revenue officers, to disqualify Government contractors from sitting in Parliament and to strike heavily at sinecures and pensions, allowed the inquiry into Parliamentary Reform as suggested by the young William Pitt on May 7, 1782, to

4

be defeated by 161 votes against 141. Exactly a year later, with the Fox–North Coalition in power, Pitt suffered a much heavier reverse in a division of 293 against 149, although he now spoke not only on behalf of the "more moderate" agitation (portrayed in No. 8) but as an ex-Cabinet Minister. When he re-opened the matter as Prime Minister in 1785, his very moderate Reform proposals, even though supported in the lobby by Fox, were defeated by 248 votes against 174.

For some years "parliamentary reformation" ceased to be on the Commons agenda; it was replaced in 1787 by the Protestant Dissenters' agitation to free themselves from the disabilities imposed by the Test and Corporation Acts. When Pitt, holding that these disabilities were nominal rather than real, repeatedly opposed the extension of "religious liberty", he drove some of the Dissenting leaders, notably Drs. Price and Priestley, to a much more critical attitude. After the French Revolution had begun in 1789, it was Dr. Price who became its first notorious panegyrist and who called for the political and religious enfranchisement of Britain to the same extent as had just been found proper in France. In 1790 when repeal of the Test Act and Parliamentary Reform were both pressed in Parliament, Pitt, already much influenced by Burke's passionate hostility to the results of mob-power in Paris, helped to secure their rejection. In November 1790, the anti-revolutionary passion that Burke had already thrown into Parliamentary debate, was repeated for all the world to read in his famous *Reflections on the French Revolution*.

It was one of the critics of Burke, Tom Paine, who in publishing two parts of the *Rights of Man* in 1791 and 1792, issued what proved to be the principal inspiring force of working-class Radicalism for the next half-century. Paine was a pamphleteer of rare force and experience, who had worked with his hands before taking to the pen and could accurately gauge the temper of the "intelligent" handicraftsman or small tradesman. Here is a characteristic passage on the origins of monarchy and aristocracy from the *Rights of Man*:

> It could have been no difficult thing in the early and solitary ages of the world, while the chief employment of men was that of attending flocks and herds, for a banditti of ruffians to overrun a country and lay it under contributions. Their power being thus established, the chief of the band contrived to lose the name of Robber in that of Monarch; and hence the origin of Monarchy and Kings.
>
> The origin of the government in England, so far as it relates to what is called its line of monarchy, being one of the latest, is, perhaps the best recorded. The hatred which the Norman invasion and tyranny begat, must have been deeply rooted in the nation, to have outlived the contrivance to obliterate it. Though not a courtier will talk of the curfeu-bell, not a village in England has forgotten.

And here is what Paine proposed, in Part 2, to do for the poor (and the ratepayer) by diverting, in their interest, four of the seventeen millions of annual revenue, hitherto misspent, according to him, on excessive Court, official and armament expenditure:

> First, Abolition of two million poor-rates.
> Secondly, Provision for two hundred and fifty-two thousand poor families.
> Thirdly, Education for one million and thirty thousand children.
> Fourthly, Comfortable provision for one hundred and forty thousand aged persons.
> Fifthly, Donation of twenty shillings each for fifty thousand births.

Sixthly, Donation of twenty shillings each for twenty thousand marriages.

Seventhly, Allowance of twenty thousand pounds for the funeral expenses of persons travelling for work, and dying at a distance from their friends.

Eighthly, Employment, at all times, for the casual poor in the cities of London and Westminster.

"Radical reform" occurs with increasing frequency as the aim of those students of Paine, who manned the successive agitations, repressed by the coercive measures of 1794, 1795, 1797, 1799, 1801, 1817 and 1819. By 1820, in fact, Radical Reformer and even Radical, by itself, were becoming definite party-names, and though Ministerial writers would have liked them to convey to the ordinary citizen a shocking sense of debased and predatory mobs, led by blood-thirsty Jacobins of the Paine school of Republican "atheism", they greatly overplayed their hand. If Cobbett, for example, was a Radical; if Burdett, Joseph Hume and a slowly increasing part of the Parliamentary Opposition were Radical too; if Bentham, James Mill and their following were also taking to Radicalism; and if, finally, Daniel O'Connell and the discontented Catholics of Ireland were doing Radicalism's work across the Irish Sea, then Radicalism soon bade fair to dominate the United Kingdom. In 1832, indeed, it seemed for a short time as though some such development might be on the way, although by that time even the Tory alarmists, who counted the number of "Radicals" returned to the first reformed Parliament as 190, were prepared to admit that they were sub-divided into quite a number of categories: leaders of the Political Unions of 1831–2, followers of Hume or Cobbett, O'Connell's "tail", or mere time-serving Whig-Radicals who would desert at the first opportunity. In point of fact, the "Parliamentary Radicals", as they were soon called, though an important force for compelling the Whig Front Bench to attempt, between 1833 and 1841, critical changes in the Church, the Corporations, Ireland and the Empire, in the teeth of the Lords, were rarely, if ever, able to raise fifty votes for a course that might have involved a complete breach with the Whigs.

Out-of-doors, meanwhile, the Ultra-Radicalism was developing which became the Chartist Universal Suffrage movement of 1838–48. The Parliamentary Radicals of the time put the immediate possibilities, of course, a good deal lower than the Chartists' Six Points, even if there was a disciplined and united agitation which carefully refrained from every unnecessary antagonisation of the "public". The abolition of members' property qualifications did not, in fact, come till 1858; a limited Householder Suffrage, confined to the boroughs, not till the Second Reform Bill of 1867; and Vote by Ballot not till 1872.

Alongside the main Suffrage struggle for the legislative machinery of the State, many collateral campaigns were conducted for "radical reform" of other points of the social and political system. The best-remembered is the campaign for Repeal of the Corn and Provision Laws which was decided when a Tory Prime Minister, who had already made important concessions, undertook Corn Law Repeal in 1846 with the help of the Whig and Radical Opposition. A more exhausting struggle, in some ways, had to be waged for over three decades before Dissenters were freed from Compulsory Church Rates in 1868. Disestablishment and partial Disendowment of the Church of England in Ireland was not achieved until 1869, and the abolition of Anglican Tests at the Universities not till 1871. But even these changes left Dissenters with alleged grievances of every kind that made them the backbone of the Radical electorate to 1914 and even beyond.

Very often the Dissenting grievance coincided with a democratic working-class objection to things as they were, and then the "millions" were frequently won for a powerful agitation that finally compelled legislation. In the bitter Education controversies that often raged between Dissenters and Churchmen, a good deal of working-class support normally went to the Dissenters as against an "aristocratic" and "privileged" Church which did not scruple, it was claimed, to demand ever-increasing help for its schools and training colleges from the taxes and, finally, from the rates. If the School Boards were one of the principal spheres in which a Radical alliance was relatively easy to make between Dissenters and "working-man" representatives, there were other local government spheres, too, in which similar alliances could set to work on a Radical programme. Until 1889 the County magistrates' benches, with a property qualification and over-whelmingly Anglican in composition, controlled both County Administration and judicature; the County Councils Act of 1888, substituting elected County Councils for the magistrates in administrative matters, had been demanded by radical reformers for decades. The democratisation of smaller local government bodies, as carried out by the Local Government Act of 1894, represented another long Radical crusade carried to victory. No longer would the Anglican incumbent preside in the Parish Vestry as *ex officio* Chairman, flanked by his Churchwardens, while plural voting, which had hitherto allowed some wealthy resident property-owners up to twelve times the voting power of the smaller ratepayers, would cease to be possible in Parish, District and Poor Law Union elections.

The voting position at Parliamentary elections had meanwhile been democratised by the Reform Bill of 1884 and the Redistribution Act of 1885, The further "Radical Programme", however, for reclaiming from landowners some rights in the land for the "people", lost its chance when the "party of progress" split on Home Rule for Ireland and encountered the electoral disaster of 1886. A new and vaster Radical programme was devised in 1891 as the "Newcastle Programme", but though it just allowed the electoral scales to be turned in 1892, it, too, proved almost completely incapable of being carried out when politics became engulfed in a new Home Rule dispute, followed by another Conservative triumph in 1895. It took ten years of Conservative mistakes, especially in regard to "Imperialism", to make possible the great Radical electoral triumphs of January 1906. One very characteristic result was the Act of 1906 which, at last, abolished the property qualification for County magistrates. In 1907 there followed the first Budget discrimination between earned and unearned income, and in 1908 the Old Age Pensions Act, partly made possible by that discrimination.

The holders of the great inherited incomes, many of them derived from land, had not ventured to destroy, through their control of the House of Lords, either the Income Tax change of 1907 or the Old Age Pensions Act of 1908. They were biding their time and, meanwhile, they did their best to humiliate the "Radical"

Government by wrecking its attempted Education and Liquor legislation, the unpopular products, it was claimed, of Dissenting rancour and Teetotal fanaticism. Then came the great struggle of 1909–10 on the "People's Budget", regarded as the first step in a new Radical campaign against the landowners, and the further struggle of 1910–11 on the Parliament Act, which so much reduced the power of the Lords. The elections of January and December 1910, which decided these struggles, left Liberal and Radical groups of professional and business men still the central core of a shrunken House of Commons majority, obtained by working alliances with Irish Nationalists impatient for Home Rule, and a British Labour party impatient to take over the government itself as the true representative of the "toiling millions". "Labour's" impatience was met, to some extent, by carrying Payment of Members in 1911 and by adding to the Trade Disputes Act of 1906 the Trade Union Act of 1912 to legalise the political activities and the political levies of the Trade Unions. And the Irish Nationalist alliance against the Tories was retained by introducing a Home Rule Bill in 1912 which, under the Government's tactical plans, was to be carried, accompanied by Welsh Disestablishment and a Bill against Plural Voting, through the three Sessions of 1912, 1913 and 1914. Under the Parliament Act, all three measures would then become law despite rejection by the House of Lords.

It was recognised that to carry three such contentious measures as Home Rule, Welsh Disestablishment, and the Plural Voting Bill, without a special mandate from the "people", gave the Conservative Opposition a strong moral case for prolonged resistance. But the

Home Rule Bill was resisted in Ulster by more than words, and the Plural Voting Bill aroused forceful opposition from the Suffragettes because women's claims to the vote were left unrecognised. The original draft of the Plural Voting Bill, however, was at first regarded as likely to secure a prolongation of Radical control of the Commons, since it proposed the end of University representation, the end of the rich or business man's plural voting, and several other ways of establishing the allegedly ideal democracy, based on the principle of " one man, one vote ". At the same time a new anti-landlord campaign was being launched, calculated, it was hoped, to help the Plural Voting Bill to give " advanced Liberalism " and Radicalism a prolongation of power at the General Election, due in 1915.

No General Election, however, took place in 1915 because of the outbreak of the Great War of 1914–18. And when the General Election did at last come in 1918, the Asquith–Lloyd George feud had fatally split the dominant Radical groups of 1906–14. The immediate gainer seemed to be Conservatism, but Labour's absorption of Radical politicians and Radical voters went on so fast that the first Labour Government was formed in 1924 and the second in 1929. Before long the very name of Radical appeared to have become obsolete in England, the land of its birth, though it still commanded extensive allegiance elsewhere. The final die was cast when, after five years of persistent and able effort between 1924 and 1929, Lloyd George's attempt to recapture working-class confidence from the Labour party failed. Yet the Radical programme, which Lloyd George had imposed on a not altogether willing Liberal Party, was proved by later events to have had greater immediate prospects than Labour's of averting the mass unemployment of ensuing years.

British Radicalism's fate had, of course, been decided by developments working themselves out long before the actual polls which registered it during the 1920s. One cause, in fact, was Radicalism's own success in getting the gradual removal of the most obviously unjustifiable and anachronistic legacies of the past. When something approaching Universal Male Suffrage had been obtained in 1884, Radicalism was in danger of losing its main justification for existence unless it could convert the Liberals into a Social Reform party with "equality of opportunity for all" far more fundamentally interpreted than hitherto, and with the abolition of hunger and distress as another immediate objective. Joseph Chamberlain, who saw the need and was probably of the calibre to meet it, might well have come to dominate national politics with a Radical policy thus fundamentally re-interpreted and imposed on the Liberal Party.

But Chamberlain left the "party of progress" in 1886. Its Radical "faddists and crocheteers" misinterpreted and wasted their chances of 1892–95, and Radicalism might well have begun a gradual exit from history but for the fact that it still provided the main opportunities of opposition to the South African and Tariff bungling of the entrenched Conservatism of 1895–1905. But there were critics who recognised, on the very eve of the sweeping Radical victories of January 1906, that Radicalism's risks of passing into obsolescence were growing and that, in the picturesque phrase of Cecil Chesterton, it was dominated not merely by the "ghosts" of Gladstone and of Cobden but even by the remoter ghosts of the Puritans and of

Calvin. In fact, what the "enthusiastic Radical" imagined to be "the very latest manifestations of progressive thought" could be dismissed as originating in nothing more relevant than a series of out-of-date antipathies: "a prejudice against peers (though not against capitalists), a prejudice against religious establishments, a prejudice against state interference with *foreign* trade . . . a prejudice against Imperialism, a prejudice against what is vaguely called 'militarism' —that is to say against provision for national defence. Add prejudices borrowed from the Nonconformists against publicans and priests and you have the sum total . . . the refuse of a dead epoch and an exploded theory of politics".[1]

This confident and destructive criticism of the Radicalism of 1905 came from a Fabian Socialist, anxious to hasten the process by which working-class leaders and their Trade Unions were "emancipating" themselves from the Radical tradition and adopting Socialism. What, in fact, happened was something more complicated. With Trade Union backing, "Labour leaders" came forward in increasing numbers as Parliamentary candidates, but their Election Addresses, though giving greater prominence, of course, to the claims of the poor and the Trade Unions, largely echoed the Radical case on Free Trade, South Africa, and the Tory Education and Licensing Acts. Gradually the typical Labour Address came to shed these topics and to introduce Socialist themes from the ample and systematic propaganda of the Fabians. The Fabians were the most respectable and disarming of Socialists; they had no use for bloodshed or armed revolution; they allowed for some compensation to expropriated

[1] Cecil Chesterton's *Gladstonian Ghosts* (1905), pp. 32–33.

14

capitalists and landlords; and their paper Paradises seemed quite credibly arranged even if there was some evasion of the central problem of production incentives.

Whether Radicalism, re-popularised by the " People's Budget " and the platform feats of Lloyd George, could now have staved off the " advance of Socialism " for any length of time is most doubtful. The flood of confident Socialist Utopianism was too strong to be dammed. As it was, war conditions between 1914 and 1918 increased the demands and expectations of the most Socialist of the workers, and Lloyd George's alliance with the Conservatives between 1916 and 1922, ended any attractions his personality might have had for millions of voters to whom his Radical programmes of 1924–29 might, otherwise, have made some appeal. In 1929 it became obvious that the heirs of Owen and Marx had displaced those of Price and Cartwright in the leadership of the " millions ", and that large-scale experiments with State Socialism would be persistently advocated. Inevitable, too, appeared the complete dissolution of the old Radicalism, as one body of its adherents passed into the anti-Socialist camp and another continued to join the new Radicalism, though often, it is true, with the tacit intention of moderating and guiding it (No. 76).

Part I

BEFORE THE FRENCH REVOLUTION

1763–1789

BEFORE THE FRENCH REVOLUTION

1763–1789

MODERN British Radicalism was born in the struggle of the streets against what were believed to be the sinister Palace politics of George III. The retirement of Pitt in October 1761; the virtual expulsion of Newcastle in May 1762 to make way for Bute; and the signing of an unpopular peace all served as grounds for a war of pamphlet, caricature and mob demonstration against the influences supposedly reigning at Court, a war which reached hitherto unparalleled depths of scurrility and irresponsibility.

For a number of reasons the Court and Ministry chose to make their main counter-attack on No. 45 of the *North Briton*. But there was considerable bungling and miscalculation in their issue and execution of the general warrant of April 26, 1763, since forty-eight people, many of them innocent of all connection with the incriminated libels, were arrested in company with Wilkes, the Member of Parliament responsible. Wilkes, able to pose as a hero defending both liberty of the subject and liberty of the Press against Court encroachments, won enormous popularity with the mob. Ministers found, indeed, the means of disgracing Wilkes late in 1763, but they disgraced themselves almost as much in the process, so that Wilkes's political letters from the Continent, where he took refuge until the General Election of the spring of 1768, had their importance and certainly served to keep vivid memories of him alive. Huge mobs of the unenfranchised saw to it, almost by main force, that he was elected M.P. for Middlesex in 1768 and was re-elected three times in 1769 when the Court and Parliamentary majority undertook his expulsion.

The Court and Parliamentary majority finally seated another in Wilkes's place in spite of his only having received 296 votes against Wilkes's 1,143. But a long-sustained outburst of public anger followed, and during its course an important agitation was undertaken by what may be counted as the first real Radical organisation, the Society of Supporters of the Bill of Rights, founded in February 1769. This society was soon stimulating petitions calling for the dissolution of the " corrupt Parliament " which, under improper influence, had unseated Wilkes, defied the electorate and broken the Constitution.[1] The weaknesses of Wilkes's private character eventually broke the agitators into two groups, and the famous " Parson Horne " (Horne Tooke) became the guiding spirit of another society, sometimes called the Constitutional Society, which, like the original society, demanded a " reformation " of Parliament which would assure the country " a just and equal representation ".

George III's Ministers, while struggling with a new type of popular opposition at home, had also been set the problem of dealing with an insurrectionary popular opposition in America (No. 3). Though it was Wilkes, too, who became, in Parliament, the most outright defender of the Americans, it is a famous pamphleteering effort of the Dissenting leader, Dr.

---

[1] The foundation announcement of the Bill of Rights Society, and extracts from one of the petitions which it promoted are given below (Nos. 1 and 2). Wilkes's speech on Parliamentary Reform, made in 1776, is quoted in No. 5.

Richard Price, which is used below (No. 4) to illustrate the sour anti-Ministerial temper prevalent among the large sections of the trading and commercial classes which were influenced by chapel pulpits traditionally suspicious of the ways of Courts and Kings. It is worth noting that Price's *Observations on the Nature of Civil Liberty, the Principles of Government, and the Justice and Policy of the War with America* won an immense sale, probably unprecedented for the time.[1]

Meanwhile, the steadily increasing taxation made necessary by the long American struggle inclined more and more people to study the advantages which " parliamentary reformation " might bring if it permitted the ending of such parliaments as had (so it was argued) been influenced, corrupted and bribed into forcing war upon the Americans. An extract is given from John Cartwright's *Legislative Rights of the Commonality Vindicated* of 1777 (No. 6), to indicate the very radical parliamentary reform that was already being suggested. By 1780, the heavy and continuing burden of a war that had now allied France and Spain with the Americans, and threatened to ally others too, called out a famous " Oeconomy " movement, whose leaders demanded an end of the numerous sinecures which, apart from being an expense in themselves, had provided Crown and Ministry with a great part of the means of " influencing " Parliament towards the disastrous American war. An extreme wing of the " Oeconomy " movement went so far as to claim that nothing less than Universal Suffrage, Annual Parliaments, and more, could eradicate corruption, arrest the swift descent to ruin, and restore the pristine virtues of

---

[1] See also the volume by Max Beloff in this series: *The Debate on the American Revolution.*

the British Constitution. If there were the space, the *Report of the Sub-Committee of Westminster* (No. 7), dated May 27, 1780, would be well worth printing in full as by far the most advanced political programme produced in eighteenth-century Britain before the French Revolution. On the purely political side, it out-distanced many Radical programmes even of the nineteenth century and anticipated all six points of the "People's Charter".

A Reform programme that came a good deal nearer to the immediate "practical politics" of 1780 than the Westminster Report was that developed almost simultaneously by an association composed of the many Yorkshire landowners, clergymen, and professional men who had begun the original "Oeconomy" movement in 1779 under the skilful leadership of a well-known Yorkshire landowner and cleric, the Rev. Mr. Wyvill. There is ample evidence of Wyvill's skill in the manifesto (No. 8), issued by his associates late in 1781, after difficult yet fruitful negotiations with other associations erected on the Yorkshire model. As these negotiations led on to Pitt's Reform motions of 1782 and 1783, and these, in turn, to the Reform Bill of 1785, Wyvill's place in the line of English Reformers is secure.

1 : FOUNDATION ANNOUNCEMENT OF THE SOCIETY OF SUPPORTERS OF THE BILL OF RIGHTS, 1769

LONDON TAVERN
February 25, 1769

MANY gentlemen, members of Parliament and others, divested of every personal consideration, and unconnected with any party, have formed themselves into a Society at the London Tavern, under the title of Supporters of the Bill of Rights. Their sole aim is to maintain and defend the legal, constitutional liberty of the subject. They mean to support Mr. Wilkes and his cause, as far as it is a public cause. For this purpose they solicit the countenance and encouragement of the public, whose advantage and emolument alone are intended.

(*The Controversial Letters of Wilkes and Horne*, 1771, pp. 150–151)

2: The humble Address, Remonstrance, and Petition of the Electors of the City and Liberty of Westminster, assembled in Westminster Hall, the 28th of March, 1770

We, your majesty's most dutiful and loyal subjects . . . having already presented our humble but ineffectual application to the throne, find ourselves, by the misconduct of your majesty's ministers, in confederacy with many of our representatives, reduced to the necessity of again breaking in by our complaints upon your majesty's repose . . .

By the same secret and unhappy influence to which all our grievances have been originally owing, the redress of those grievances has now been prevented . . . with this additional circumstance of aggravation, that while the invaders of our rights remain the directors of your majesty's councils, the defenders of those rights have been dismissed from your majesty's service . . .

We beg leave, therefore, again to represent to your majesty, that the House of Commons have struck at

23

the most valuable liberties and franchises of all the electors of Great Britain . . . by assuming to themselves a right of chusing, instead of receiving a member when chosen . . .

We presume again therefore humbly to implore from your majesty, the only remedies which are in any way proportioned to the nature of the evil: that you would be graciously pleased to dismiss for ever from your councils, those ministers who are ill suited by their dispositions to preserve the principles of a free, or by their capacities to direct the councils, of a great and mighty kingdom . . .

And that by speedily dissolving the present parliament, your majesty will shew by your own example, and by their dissolution, that the rights of your people are to be inviolable . . .

We find ourselves compelled to urge with the greater importunity, this our humble but earnest application to the throne, as every day seems to produce the confirmation of some old, or to threaten the introduction of some new injury. We have the strongest reasons to apprehend, that the usurpation begun by the House of Commons upon the right of electing, may be extended to the right of petitioning; and that under the pretence of restraining the abuse of this right, it is meant . . . to intimidate us from the exercise of the right itself . . .

We rely therefore upon the royal word . . . that our grievances will meet with full redress, and our complaints with the most favourable interpretation.

(*The Gentleman's Magazine*, March 1770)

3 : THE MIDDLESEX ELECTION OF 1774, AND WILKES'S NOMINATION AS LORD MAYOR OF LONDON

SEPTEMBER 26TH. At a meeting of the freeholders at Mile-End assembly-room, agreeable to an advertisement of the sheriffs, for the nomination of two fit and proper persons to represent the county of Middlesex, Mr. Serjeant Glynn and Mr. John Wilkes were almost unanimously approved, there being only four objectors to Mr. Wilkes's nomination. They afterwards signed the following engagement:

We, (J. Wilkes and J. Glynn Esqrs.) do solemnly promise and engage ourselves to our constituents, if we have the honour to be chosen the representatives of the county of Middlesex, that we will endeavour to the utmost of our power, to restore and defend the excellent form of government modelled and established at the revolution, and to promote acts of the legislature for shortening the duration of parliaments, for excluding placemen and pensioners from the House of Commons; for a more fair and equal representation of the people; for vindicating the injured rights of the freeholders of this county, and the whole body of the electors of this united kingdom; and an act for the repeal of the four late acts respecting America; the Quebec act, establishing popery, and the system of French Canadian laws, in that extensive province; the Boston port-act, the act for altering the charter of the province of Massachusett's-Bay, and the act for the trial, in Europe, of persons accused of criminal offences in America; being fully persuaded, that the passing of such acts will be of the utmost importance for the security of our excellent constitution, and the restoration of the rights and liberties of our fellow-subjects in America.

OCTOBER 8TH. The sheriffs came on the hustings at Guild-hall, when the Common Serjeant declared the state of the poll for Lord Mayor for the year ensuing to be, For John Wilkes, Esq. 1957; The Rt. Hon. Fred. Bull 1923; Sir James Esdaile 1474; Alderman Kennet 1410 . . .
The sheriffs then returned to the Court of Aldermen, and in about an hour afterwards they again returned . . . when the Recorder . . . stood up, and declared the election of the Court of Aldermen, for a Lord Mayor . . . for the year ensuing, to have fallen on John Wilkes Esq.

(*The Annual Register,* 1774)

4 : RICHARD PRICE: *Observations on the Nature of Civil Liberty, the Principles of Government, and the Justice and Policy of the War with America,* 1776 (pp. 93–99)

THE general cry was last winter, that the people of New England were a body of cowards, who would at once be tumbled into submission by a hostile look from our troops. In this light they were held up to public derision in both Houses of Parliament . . . Indeed no one can doubt but that had it been believed some time ago that the people of America were *brave*, more care would have been taken not to provoke them . . .
Again, the manner in which this war has been hitherto conducted, renders it still more disgraceful . . . English valour being thought insufficient to subdue the

26

Colonies, the laws and religion of *France* were established in *Canada*, on purpose to obtain the power of bringing upon them from thence an army of *French Papists*. The wild *Indians* and their own slaves have been instigated to attack them: and attempts have been made to gain the assistance of a large body of *Russians*. With like views, *German* troops have been hired: and the defence of our Forts and Garrisons trusted in their hands . . . If, indeed, our ministers can at any time, without leave, not only send away the national troops, but introduce *foreign* troops in their room, we lie entirely at mercy, and we have everything to dread . . .

In this hour of tremendous danger, it would become us to turn our thoughts to Heaven. This is what our brethren in the Colonies are doing. From one end of North America to the other, they are FASTING and PRAYING. But what are we doing? Shocking thought! we are ridiculing them as *Fanatics*, and scoffing at religion. We are running wild after pleasure, and forgetting everything serious and decent at *Masquerades*. We are gambling in gaming houses: trafficking for Boroughs: perjuring ourselves at Elections: and selling ourselves for places—which side then is Providence likely to favour? In *America* we see a number of rising states in the vigour of youth, inspired by the noblest of all passions, the passion for being free; and animated by piety. *Here* we see an old state, great indeed, but inflated and irreligious; enervated by luxury: encumbered with debts; and hanging by a thread. Can any one look without pain to the issue? May we not expect calamities? . . .

Is our cause such as gives us reason to ask God to bless it? Can we in the face of Heaven declare, " that we are not the aggressors in this war: and that we mean by it, not to acquire or even preserve dominion for its own sake; not conquest or Empire, or the gratification of resentment, but solely to deliver ourselves from oppression; to gain reparation for injury: and to defend ourselves against men who would plunder or kill us?" Remember, reader, whoever thou art, that there are no other just causes of war; and that blood spilled, with any other views, must some time or other be accounted for . . .

5: John Wilkes's Speech in Parliament upon Parliamentary Reform, March 21, 1776

VOTES OF MARCH 21, 1776

A MOTION was made, and the Question was put, " That leave be given to bring in a Bill, for a just and equal Representation of the People of England in Parliament ". Mr. Wilkes said,

Mr. Speaker, All wise governments, and well-regulated states, have been careful to mark and correct the various abuses, which a considerable length of time almost necessarily creates. Among these, one of the most striking and important in our country is, the present unfair and inadequate representation of the people of England in Parliament. It is now become so partial and unequal from the lapse of time, that I believe almost every gentleman in the House will agree with me in the necessity of its being taken into our most serious consideration . . . It appears, sir, from the writs remaining in the King's Remembrancer's office in the Exchequer that no less than 22 towns sent members to the Parliament in the 23rd, 25th, and 26th, of Edward I which have long ceased to be represented.

The names of some of them are scarcely known to us, such as those of Canebrig and Bamburg in Northumberland, Pershore and Brem in Worcestershire, Jarvall and Tykhull in Yorkshire. What a happy fate, sir, has attended the boroughs of Gatton and Old Sarum, of which, although *ipsae periere ruinae*, the names are familiar to us, the clerk regularly calls them over, and four respectable gentlemen represent their departed greatness ... Great abuses, it must be owned, contrary to the primary ideas of the English constitution, were committed by our former princes, in giving the right of representation to several paltry boroughs, because the places were poor and dependent on them, or on a favourite over-grown peer. The landmarks of the constitution have often been removed. The marked partiality for Cornwall, which single county still sends, within one, as many members as the whole kingdom of Scotland, is striking. It arose from yielding to the crown in tin and lands a larger hereditary revenue than any other English county, as well as from the duchy being in the crown, and giving an amazing command and influence. By such abuses of our princes the constitution was wounded in its most vital part. Henry VIII restored two members, Edward VI twenty, Queen Mary four, Queen Elizabeth twelve, James I sixteen, Charles I eighteen, in all seventy-two. The alterations by creation in the same period were more considerable, for Henry VIII created thirty-three, Edward VI twenty-eight, Queen Mary seventeen, Queen Elizabeth twelve, James I eleven; in all 137 ... I am satisfied, sir, the sentiments of the people cannot be justly known at this time from the resolutions of a Parliament, composed as the present is, even though no undue influence was practiced after the return of the members to the House, even supposing for a moment the influence of all the baneful arts of corruption to be suspended, which, for a moment, I believe, they have not been under the present profligate administration.

. . . From the majority of electors only in the boroughs, which return members to this House, it has been demonstrated that this number of 254 members elected by no more than 5,723 persons, generally the inhabitants of Cornish, and other very insignificant boroughs . . . Are these the men to give laws to this vast empire, and to tax this wealthy nation? I do not mention all the tedious calculations, because gentlemen may find them at length in the works of the incomparable Dr. Price, in Postlethwaite, and in Burgh's Political Disquisitions . . . Lord Chancellor Talbot supposed the majority of this House was elected by 50,000 persons, and he exclaimed against the injustice of that idea. More accurate calculations than his Lordship's, and the unerring rules of political arithmetic, have shown the injustice to be vastly beyond what his Lordship even suspected . . .

The Americans with great reason insist, that the present war is carried on, contrary to the sense of the nation, by a ministerial junto, and an arbitrary faction, equally hostile to the rights of Englishmen and the claims of Americans. The various addresses to the throne from most numerous bodies, praying that the sword may be returned to the scabbard, and all hostilities cease, confirm this assertion . . . Our history furnishes frequent instances of the sense of Parliament running directly counter to the sense of the nation. It was notoriously of late the case in the business of the Middlesex election. I believe the fact to be equally certain in the grand American dispute, at least as to the actual hostilities now carrying on against our brethren and fellow-subjects. The proposition before us will bring the case to an issue, and from a fair and equal representation of the people, America may at length distinguish the real sentiments of freemen and Englishmen.

I do not mean, sir, at this time, to go into a tedious detail of all the various proposals, which have been made for redressing this irregularity in the representation of the people . . . I will at this time, sir, only throw out general ideas, that every free agent in this kingdom should, in my wish, be represented in Parliament; that the metropolis, which contains in itself a ninth part of the people, and the counties of Middlesex, York, and others, which so greatly abound with inhabitants, should receive an increase in their representation; that the mean, and insignificant boroughs, so emphatically stiled *the rotten part of our constitution*, should be lopped off, and the electors in them thrown into the counties; and the rich, populous, trading towns, Birmingham, Manchester, Sheffield, Leeds and others, be permitted to send deputies to the great council of the nation.

The disfranchising of the mean, venal, and dependent boroughs would be laying the axe to the root of corruption and treasury influence, as well as aristocratical tyranny . . . I wish, sir, an English Parliament to speak the free, unbiased sense of the body of the English people, and of every man among us . . . The meanest mechanic, the poorest peasant and day-labourer, has important rights respecting his personal liberty, that of his wife and children, his property, however inconsiderable, his wages, his earnings, the very price and value of each day's hard labour, which are in many trades and manufactures regulated by the power of Parliament . . . Some share therefore in the power of making those laws, which deeply interest them, and to which they are expected to pay obedience, should be reserved even to this inferior, but most useful set of men in the community. We ought always to remember this important truth, acknowledged by every free state, that all government is instituted for the good of the mass of the people to be governed; that they are the original fountain of power, *and even of revenue*, and in all events the last resource . . .

(From *Wilkes's Speeches in Parliament*, 1777, Vol. I, p. 85 sqq.)

6: JOHN CARTWRIGHT: *Legislative Rights of the Commonalty Vindicated*, 1777 (2nd ed., p. 104 et sqq.)

SUFFERING as we do, from a deep parliamentary corruption, it is no time to tamper with silly correctives, and trifle away the life of public freedom: but we must go to the bottom of the stinking sore and cleanse it thoroughly: we must once more infuse into the constitution the vivifying spirit of liberty and expel the very last dregs of this poison. *Annual parliaments* with an *equal representation of the commons* are the only specifics in this case: and they would effect a radical cure. That a house of commons, formed as ours is, should maintain septennial elections, and laugh at every other idea is no wonder. The wonder is, that the British nation which, but the other day, was the greatest nation on earth, should be so easily laughed out of its liberties . . .

That man amongst the opposition to the present ruinous men and measures of the court, who shall not immediately pledge himself to the public, by the most explicit declarations and the most sacred assurances, to exert himself to the utmost of his powers and abilities . . . in attempting to bring about a thorough and compleat parliamentary reformation: and shall not instantly set about it, in preference to every other consideration, is in my opinion, nothing better than a factious demagogue: who cares not that his country be sunk in the pit of perdition, so long as he can but hope to come in for a share of power and plunder . . .

Those who now claim the *exclusive* right of sending to parliament the 513 representatives for about six millions of souls (amongst whom are one million five hundred thousand males, *competent as electors*) consist of about two hundred and fourteen thousand persons; and 254 of these representatives are elected by 5,723 . . . Their pretended rights are many of them, derived from *royal favour*; some from antient usage and prescription; and some indeed from act of parliament; but neither the most authentic acts of royalty, nor precedent, nor prescription, nor even parliament can establish any flagrant injustice; much less can they strip one million two hundred and eighty six thousand of an inalienable right, to vest it in a number amounting to only one seventh of that multitude . . .

'Tis no answer to me to say, that we have not *yet* a bastile and lettres de cachet—that we are not *yet* draughted by poll and converted into the machines of war and the military instruments of despotism by a royal mandate . . . that our courts of justice are not *yet* become courts of inquisition nor relapsed into star chambers; that the *three* branches of the legislature

33

are not *yet* become *one* in *form*, whatever they may be in effect. For all these favourable circumstances will quickly and necessarily melt away, so long as there is no power left in the hands of the people for upholding the defence of their liberty: and tyrannical doctrines and practices will as rapidly and necessarily grow into the constitution . . .

I know full well, how much the vicious part of every community affect to treat plans of reformation as chimerical—as romantic and utterly impracticable. And I know too, that the reforming of our parliamentary jurisprudence hath been particularly scoffed at, as the visionary scheme of refining system-makers and ignorant enthusiasts . . . But I regard not the clamours of the harpies: and I despise their nonsense as sincerely as I abhor their principles . . .

7: REPORT OF THE SUB-COMMITTEE OF WESTMINSTER, APPOINTED APRIL 12, 1780, TO TAKE INTO CONSIDERATION . . . THE ELECTION OF MEMBERS OF PARLIAMENT

FREE-MASONS-TAVERN

May 27, 1780

THE sub-committee having duly examined the various statutes of this realm respecting the election of members to serve in the commons' house of parliament, more particularly such as were enacted for the purpose of guarding against the prevalence of bribery and corruption at elections, and the operation of every other species of undue influence upon the electors and the elected; and reflecting upon the inefficacy of these provisions with respect to the prevention of evils, which threaten the final extinction of our liberties, are decidedly of opinion, that no effectual reformation of the abuses in question can take place, unless the people exercise their inherent and undoubted right of reviewing the whole plan of delegation . . .

Application to the crown to suspend the exertion of its influence, or to repair the breaches made in that part of the constitution, which was intended to be the bulwark of the people against its encroachments, presupposes such an ignorance of the principles, which, in certain circumstances, are found invariably to actuate the human heart, that one would be led to imagine the use of argument would be superseded by the obvious absurdity of the expedient.

The event of the experiment, frequently repeated, has confirmed the conclusion which right reason would have suggested; and it now stands a truth, recorded for the benefit of every future generation, that when the point in question is a redress of grievances, originating in oppression, or a restitution of the rights and privileges of the people, millions sue in vain.

To what earthly tribunal, therefore, shall an injured people have resort in this alarming moment, when a desperate faction, in the midst of public calamity and distress, has manifested a determined purpose of persevering in a line of conduct, which, if persisted in, must inevitably end in the subversion of our liberties, and the desolation of our state? The sun of England's glory perhaps soon may set to rise no more!

One hope still remains in the native energy of the great collective body of the people, the native energy of a race of men, who have always stood distinguished in the annals of nations for every liberal sentiment, and every generous principle that can dignify our kind.

The peaceful efforts of this mighty power, acting by committees freely chosen, are sufficient, under the providence of heaven, to re-establish the constitution in its ancient vigour . . .

When we cast our eyes upon the conduct of the present commons' house of parliament; when we behold a majority of its members, in defiance of our petitions, and their own solemn declaration, persist in increasing the burdens of the people, and in a stedfast purpose of opposing every measure of redress, desponding apprehensions may, for a time, take place in the minds of the best and bravest of our countrymen. Reflection, however, will disclose a more pleasing prospect arising from the very extremity of our distress: more vigorous counsels, and an happy unanimity will be the unavoidable result; the alarm of the nobility for the very existence of their present splendid distinctions will co-operate with the poignant feelings of the people; and every rank and description of men will feel the propriety, the necessity of establishing that plan of parliamentary reformation, which holds forth our best, and indeed our only security, against the all-devouring influence of the crown . . .

An equal representation of the people in the great council of the nation, annual elections, and the universal right of suffrage, appear so reasonable to the natural feelings of mankind, that no sophistry can elude the force of the arguments which are urged in their favour; and they are rights of so transcendent a nature, that, in opposition to the claim of the people to their enjoyment, the longest period of prescription is pleaded in vain. They were substantially enjoyed in the times of the immortal Alfred; they were cherished by the wisest princes of the Norman line; they form the grand palladium of our nation; they ought not to be esteemed the grant of royal favour, nor were they at first extorted by violence from the hand of power: they are the birthright of englishmen, their best inheritance . . .

With regard to the restitution of the universal right of suffrage the sub-committee conceive, that the reasonableness and expediency of the measure will probably be more apparent, if the full extent and magnitude of those powers be considered, which are entrusted to the representative by the constituent body.

The doctrine that representation and taxation are inseparable, is founded in truth; but the undue preference that has been afforded to the rights of property, in various discussions of the subject, has tended to keep out of sight other principles, equally essential to a just conception of the question.

A portion of the soil, a portion of its produce may be wanting to many; but every man has an interest in his life, his liberty, his kindred, and his country; and when laws affecting these are made by persons, to whom he hath not delegated the power, each of these possessions . . . may be invaded, and probably would be invaded by those, who, being possessed of property, the grand enchantress of the world, would thereby be enabled more successfully to gratify that lust of despotic power, which so strongly characterises the human heart . . .

Governed by these considerations, the sub-committee have framed the following plan . . .

I. That each county be divided into as many districts as it is entitled to elect representatives, each district chusing one representative.

II. That the division of the county into districts be

constituted in such a manner, that each district contain nearly an equal number of males competent to vote in elections . . .

III. That the election of representatives to serve in parliament be held annually through England and Wales, upon the first tuesday in July . . .

IV. That all the male inhabitants of this country (aliens, minors, criminals, and insane persons excepted) be admitted to vote at the election . . .

V. That the number of representatives, returned by the inhabitants of each county of England and Wales, be settled for the term of seven years next ensuing, according to the following schedule, viz.

Yorkshire 46; Middlesex with London and Westminster 45; Wales with Monmouth 30; Norfolk 22; . . . Kent, Lancashire, Somerset, Suffolk, each eighteen, 72; Lincolnshire 17; Essex, Surry with Southwark, each sixteen, 32; Gloucestershire 13; Hampshire, Wilts., each eleven, 22; Cheshire, Cornwall, Derbyshire, Northamptonshire, Salop, Staffordshire, each ten, 60 . . . the counties of Huntingdon and Westmoreland, each three, 6; the county of Rutland and the two universities, each two, 6; (Total 513) . . .

IX. That the poll of each district be taken by ballot . . .

XI. That the annual session of parliament shall commence upon the first thursday in November, unless some extraordinary event, or urgent national business, should make it indisputably requisite for the crown to assemble it before the stated period . . .

XIII. That all members of the commons' house of parliament, before taking their seats, declare upon oath, that they do not hold any office or emolument at the will of the crown, or its servants, or any lord of parliament . . .

XIV. That all members serving in parliament be entitled to reasonable wages, according to the wholesome practice of ancient times . . .

XVI. That every person competent to give his suffrage as an elector, be also esteemed qualified to be elected to serve his country in parliament.

(This was drafted by Dr. John Jebb and is táken from *The Works of John Jebb, M.D., F.R.S.,* iii, p. 403 et sqq.)

8: A Second Address from the Committee of Association of the County of York to the Electors, 1781

THAT the representation of the People is extremely inadequate; that the septennial duration of Parliament is a dangerous and unwarrantable Innovation; that Corruption cannot be restrained; that our Liberties cannot be secured but by the correction of those gross abuses; these are propositions in which there is a most unanimous agreement. But whether the People should attempt to restore annual Parliaments; to extend the right of suffrage annually; and to establish a perfect equality of representation; or whether it does not behove them rather to confine their efforts to the accomplishment of a more limited plan; to shorten the duration of Parliaments to a term not exceeding three years, and to reinforce the sound part of our representation by the addition of One Hundred Members to the Counties and the Metropolis: These are questions which for some time were the subject of frequent discussion . . .

On behalf of the more extensive plan, much was urged on the true principles of Government with indefatigable zeal; and the considerations which could be drawn from the natural rights of Men and the ancient privileges of Englishmen were presented in every form of argument . . . It is indisputably true, that *annual elections* of Parliament were from the earliest times the practice of our forefathers . . . That mankind are naturally equal, is also a proposition which cannot be denied; and although wherever Society is established, the introduction of inequality in some respects, is unavoidable, yet every humane and equitable mind must disapprove invidious exclusions, by which that inequality is unnecessarily increased. The right of suffrage, though not universally, was more extensively enjoyed by our ancestors before the Reign of Henry VI than in the succeeding period: And if the manners and prejudices of the present age could admit *the restoration of that privilege* in its fullest extent, with an *annual choice of representatives*, the Advocates of the more moderate plan would rejoice at the change.

The diversity of sentiment, therefore, which has in some measure retarded the union of the people, arose, not from a difference of political principles; for in them there is an entire agreement . . . The questions in debate have been, not, whether those doctrines be maintainable in argument, for it is admitted they are; but whether it be probable in the present state of the nation, that those doctrines in their full extent, are reducible to practice? And if it be highly improbable, that a Reformation on that extensive plan could be carried into execution, whether it be not expedient that the People wave somewhat of their justifiable claims, and content themselves with that mode of Redress which is *less complete in theory*, but which appears *more easily attainable* by peaceful means, and when attained, *fully adequate* to the purpose of their opposition? . . .

The Committee of Association for the County of York have once more presumed thus freely to communicate to their Fellow Electors their sentiments on the *decline of the Constitution* and *the means of its Restoration*. From this survey of the various plans of Reformation which have been offered to the People, their choice seems wisely to have been fixed on that system in which *efficacy* and *practicability* are most advantageously combined; and in the judgement of this Committee, if that SUBSTANTIAL REDRESS cannot be obtained, the formalities of an Upper and a Lower Assembly may still be continued, but the Liberty of Britain must soon be no more . . . To rectify a disordered Legislature must indeed be a work of the greatest toil and difficulty; but there is yet in the Independent Part of the Community a fund of vigour adequate to the task; and the ancient spirit of the Constitution still affords unexhausted resources to the People, for a lawful, orderly and effectual interposition. Peaceful Association is the lawful mode adopted by this Committee, in concert with many of their countrymen; and by a steady prosecution of the *more moderate plan for the Reformation of Parliament in this mode*, they still trust the Constituent Body may regain its ascendant over the Representative Assembly. Far, therefore, from wishing to promote confusion, or to prompt their fellow-citizens to deeds of violence and desperation; they exhort them with conscientious sincerity to confine their efforts within the bounds of legality . . .

With these views the Committee of Yorkshire first

41

embarked in this cause . . . *They have been menaced by High Authority; they have been defamed by Reverend Calumny;* but conscious of the purity of their intentions, certain of the legality of their conduct, they cheerfully commit their reputation to the justice of their countrymen, AND THEIR PERSONAL SAFETY TO THE PROTECTION OF THOSE LAWS WHICH CANNOT BE INFRINGED, WITHOUT A DIRECT ASSUMPTION OF DESPOTIC POWER.

Part II

THE FRENCH REVOLUTION AND THE NAPOLEONIC WARS
1789–1815

THE FRENCH REVOLUTION AND
THE NAPOLEONIC WARS
1789–1815

WHEN the French Revolution broke out in 1789, Parliamentary Reform was something of a dead issue in British politics. For a variety of reasons—above all, perhaps, the stupid and destructive anti-Catholic rioting undertaken by the Gordon mobs of 1780—the notion of " Universal Suffrage " seemed to have become more chimerical than ever. Even Pitt's official plan, to acquire seventy-two seats for redistribution by offering to find Treasury compensation for the electors of decayed boroughs who were willing to bargain, met with a heavy defeat when introduced by the Prime Minister in 1785.

The fall of Church and State privilege in France, however, received a rapturous welcome from many Dissenting circles, and unqualified applause was given to the French Revolution by Dr. Price, one of the leaders of Dissent, in his *Discourse on the Love of our Country, delivered on November 4, 1789*. Price's sermon sold in tens of thousands of copies, but its very success spelt danger for the Dissenters, for it angered many who found Price far too ready to praise everything in revolutionary France—and America—while decrying everything British. Price's sermon was actually the occasion of Burke's great attack upon this uncritical attitude to his *Reflections.*[1]

[1] See the volume in this series by Alfred Cobban: *The Debate on the French Revolution.*

45

In 1791 Tom Paine published the most famous of the replies to Burke—the first part of his *Rights of Man*. Perhaps even more important for its influence on English Radical thought was the second part, which appeared in January 1792. For, if the first part had attacked the place taken by monarchy and aristocracy in government, the second part claimed to show how the abolition of monarchy and the imposition of a steeply graduated Income Tax (aimed particularly at the great landed estates) could be used, with cuts in armaments and sinecures, to finance an extensive scheme of tax reductions and of special benefits to the poor, including family allowances and old age pensions.

Paine's trenchant style and epoch-making proposals made a specially strong impression on the workers of the large towns and industrial districts.[1] It is hardly too much to say that working men, hitherto incapable of any political expression save mob rioting, were first stimulated to planned political activity by Paine. For, although Paine himself was soon driven abroad by a prosecution for seditious libel, the growth of working-class societies, praising the French Revolution and demanding similar radical reform in Britain, continued apace, unchecked even by the bloody September massacres in Paris, the deposition of Louis XVI, or the plain approach of an Anglo-French crisis portending war. Even when war came in February 1793 and made the selling of Paine's pamphlets, the summoning of Reform meetings, and the loan to them of public-house rooms more hazardous, activity among the Reform

[1] See No. 10, which quotes not the *Rights of Man* itself (still easily accessible in numerous reprints) but a typical communication in its praise from one of the many new Reform Societies whose creation or growth it was so powerfully stimulating. No. 11 quotes from another pamphlet of Paine's, written in 1792 and almost as incisive as the *Rights of Man* itself.

46

Societies continued on a surprising scale. In August and September 1793, two Scottish radicals, Muir and Palmer, were sentenced to fourteen and seven years transportation (No. 12). These savage sentences, however, did not prevent the organisation of a delegate convention by the Scottish radical societies at Edinburgh in November of the same year.

A bold front was assumed under the leadership of two enterprising representatives from England, Margarot and Gerald. The Assembly took on the imposing title of *The British Convention of Delegates of the People, associated to obtain Universal Suffrage and Annual Parliaments*, and was engaged in busy and confident discussion in its third week when the assembly was dispersed and its secretary, Skirving, taken into custody, with Gerald and Margarot, for the prosecution of serious charges against them. All three were sentenced to fourteen years transportation, and extracts (printed as No. 13) from the Second Report of the Committee of Secrecy, appointed by the House of Lords in May 1794, show the Government's case against them.

The Government's attempt to extend similar measures to England failed. In May 1794 a dozen leaders of the two principal Radical Associations, the London Corresponding Society and the Society for Constitutional Information, were arrested and charged with encouraging armed revolt. The juries, however, refused to convict and the prisoners (including Hardy, secretary of the London Corresponding Society; Horne Tooke, the former collaborator of Wilkes; and Thelwall, the pioneer of Radical 'lecturing') were released amid great rejoicing. In 1795 the London Corresponding Society, indeed, organised mass demonstrations against the Government and on behalf of radical reform. An *Address to the Nation*, adopted at one of these meetings, is printed as No. 14.

The Government's reply was to pass the notorious Two Acts for suppressing treasonable practices and seditious meetings. The Corresponding Society protested, but failed to arrest the Government's course. For a time, indoor meetings continued, but the popular impulse dwindled and by April 1798 when the Committee of the society was arrested, this phase of radical agitation was at an end (No. 15).

Radical activity revived in 1806, when Cobbett, already the hardest-hitting journalist of the time, completed his conversion to Radicalism with his *Letters to the Electors of Westminster*. In 1807 he succeeded, with the aid of such men as Francis Place (once prominent in the old London Corresponding Society), in securing Sir Francis Burdett as M.P. for Westminster.[1]

From 1807 to 1832 and beyond, Westminster, with its very wide measure of householder-enfranchisement, became the Radical headquarters of the country, and no Radical agitation would have been deemed complete without a Westminster meeting and a Westminster petition to give a lead to the rest of the country.

The sensation caused by the revelation in 1809 that the Duke of York, second son of the King and Commander-in-Chief, had allowed a mistress to traffic in military commissions proved particularly favourable to Westminster demonstrations. Accordingly, after Burdett had made his comment on the Duke of York in the Parliamentary proceedings of March 13 (a comment extensively reproduced in pamphlet form), a

[1] While Nos. 16 and 17 give typical quotations from Burdett's speeches and writing at this time, No. 21 shows the continued growth of Cobbett's influence.

great meeting of Westminster electors was summoned to Westminster Hall " to express their sentiments " and to hear Burdett and Whitbread explain why the new revelations only made plainer " the necessity of an immediate reform of the House of Commons ".

The next Westminster demonstration took the form of a great Reform banquet on May 1, attended by several members of Parliament and many provincial representatives, and during its course, Major Cartwright, the oldest campaigner for " Radical Reform " still active, was given the honour of moving the fourteen Reform Resolutions, which are printed as No. 18 partly because they sum up much else. The Resolutions were, of course, carried amid great acclamations, but when Burdett's Reform motion came on in Parliament, on June 15, the result was far from impressive, a mere vote of fifteen against the Government's majority of seventy-four.

Another picture of the Westminster Radical forces in action is worth giving. The first extravagant Corn Law ideas, mooted at a moment when the end of the Napoleonic Wars seemed about to make the import of cheap Continental corn a possibility, aroused a storm of popular hostility and had to be modified downwards. Some further modification was undertaken before Ministers at length ventured to tell the country, in February 1815, that they proposed to ban the import of foreign wheat unless and until home-grown wheat fetched eighty shillings per quarter or more. Great public anger was aroused in the towns and industrial areas, condemned even in peacetime to pay scarcity prices for their food so that landlords and " great farmers " might grow even richer than the war had already made them. A host of protest meetings was organised throughout the country, and, as previously, the Westminster meeting and the Westminster petition played a leading part in the movement. Extracts from the Westminster petitions are printed as No. 22, but, for a couple of days, the angry rioting of the Westminster "mob", which, at one stage, threatened Parliament itself, seemed much more significant. It was indeed fortunate for Ministers that the news of Napoleon's re-appearance upon the scene quickly ended the hopes of peacetime plenty that had been so widely entertained.

Documents 19 and 20 in this section are a reminder that, in moments of crisis, the City of London itself and its specially privileged institutions might be captured, as in Wilkes's day, by anti-Ministerial Radicals of the city merchant and shopkeeping communities. Thus in 1812, at a season of marked commercial difficulty, the blame for which was laid on the Government's Orders in Council on trade, City of London Radicals were able to capture a majority on the City's Common Council and take the lead in demonstrations against the Government. The City Petition of 1812 was by no means the last Radical demonstration by the City: there were to be others, most notably in 1832.

9 : RICHARD PRICE: *A Discourse on the Love of Our Country, delivered on November 4, 1789, at the Meeting House in the Old Jewry, to the Society for Commemorating the Revolution in Great Britain*

OUR first concern, as lovers of our country, must be to *enlighten* it. Why are the nations of the world so patient under despotism? Why do they crouch to tyrants, and submit to be treated as if they were a herd of cattle? Is it not because they are kept in darkness, and want knowledge. Enlighten them and you will elevate them. Shew them they are *men*, and they will act like *men*. Give them just ideas of civil government, and let them know it is an expedient for gaining protection against injury and defending their rights (See the Declaration of Rights by the National Assembly of *France*, in the Appendix), and it will be impossible for them to submit to governments which, like most of those now in the world, are usurpations on the rights of men, and little better than contrivances for enabling the *few* to oppress the *many* . . .

Civil governors are properly the servants of the public; and a King is no more than the first servant of the public, created by it, maintained by it, and responsible to it; and all the homage paid to him, is due to him on no other account than his relation to the public. His sacredness is the sacredness of the community. His authority is the authority of the community; and the term MAJESTY, which it is usual to apply to him is by no means *his own* majesty but the MAJESTY OF THE PEOPLE . . .

I would further direct you to remember, that though the Revolution (of 1688) was a just work, it was by no means a perfect work: and that all was not then gained which was necessary to put the kingdom in the secure and complete possession of the blessings of liberty. In particular you should recollect, that the toleration then obtained was imperfect. It included only those who could declare their faith in the doctrinal articles of the church of England. It has, indeed, been since extended, but not sufficiently: for there still exist penal laws on account of religious opinion which (were they carried into execution) would shut up many of our places of worship, and silence and imprison some of our ablest and best men. The TEST LAWS are also still in force and deprive of eligibility to civil and military offices all who cannot conform to the established worship. It is with great pleasure that I find that the body of Protestant Dissenters, though defeated in two late attempts to deliver their country from this disgrace to it, have determined to persevere. Should they at last succeed, they will have the satisfaction not only of removing from themselves a proscription they do not deserve, but of contributing to lessen the number of our public iniquities . . .

But the most important instance of the imperfect state in which the Revolution left our constitution, is the INEQUALITY OF OUR REPRESENTATION. I think, indeed, this defect in our constitution so gross and so palpable, as to make it excellent chiefly in form and theory. You should remember that a representation in the legislature of a kingdom is the *basis* of constitutional liberty in it, and of all legitimate government: and that without it, a government is nothing but an usurpation. When the representation is fair and equal, and at the same time vested with such powers as our House of Commons possesses, a kingdom may be said to govern itself, and consequently to possess true liberty. When the representation is partial, a kingdom possesses liberty only partially: and if extremely partial, it only gives a *semblance* of liberty: but if not only extremely partial but corruptly chosen and under corrupt influence after being chosen, it becomes a *nuisance* and produces the worst of all forms of government—a government by corruption—a government carried on and supported by spreading venality and profligacy through a kingdom. May heaven preserve this kingdom from a calamity so dreadful! It is the point of depravity to which abuses under such a government as ours naturally tend, and the last stage of national unhappiness. We are at present, I hope, at a great distance from it. But it cannot be pretended that there are no advances towards it, or that there is no reason for apprehension and alarm.

The inadequateness of the representation has been long a subject of complaint. That is, in truth, our fundamental grievance; and I do not think that any thing is much more our duty, as men who love their country, and are grateful for the Revolution, than to unite our zeal in endeavouring to get it redressed. At the time of the American war, associations were formed for this purpose in London, and other parts of the kingdom; and our present minister himself has, since that war, directed to it an effort which made him a favourite with many of us. But all attention to it now seems lost, and the probability is, that this inattention will continue, and that nothing will be done towards gaining for us this essential blessing, till some great calamity again alarms our fears, or till some great abuse of power again provokes our resentment: or, perhaps, till the acquisition of a pure and equal representation by other countries (while we are mocked with the shadow) kindles our shame . . .

You may reasonably expect that I should now close this address to you. But I cannot yet dismiss you. I must not conclude without recalling particularly to your recollection a consideration to which I have more than once alluded, and which, probably, your thoughts have all along been anticipating: a consideration with which my mind is impressed more than I can express. I mean the consideration of the favourableness of the present times to all exertions in the cause of public liberty.

What an eventful period is this! I am thankful that I have lived to it: and I could almost say, *Lord, now lettest thou thy servant depart in peace, for mine eyes have seen thy salvation.* I have lived to see a diffusion of knowledge, which has undermined superstition and error—I have lived to see the rights of man better understood than ever; and nations panting for liberty, which have seemed lost to the idea of it—I have lived to see over THIRTY MILLIONS of people, indignant and resolute, spurning at slavery, and demanding liberty with an irresistible voice: their king led in triumph and an arbitrary monarch surrendering himself to his subjects. After sharing in the benefits of one Revolution, I have been spared to be a witness to two other Revolutions, both glorious. And now, methinks, I see the ardor for liberty catching and spreading; a general amendment beginning in human affairs, the dominion of Kings changed for the dominion of laws, and the dominion of priests giving way to the dominion of reason and conscience.

Be encouraged, all ye friends of freedom and writers in its defence! The times are auspicious. Your labours have not been in vain. Behold, kingdoms, admonished by you, starting from sleep, breaking their fetters, and claiming justice from their oppressors! Behold, the light you have struck out, after setting America free, reflected to France, and there kindled into a blaze that lays despotism in ashes, and warms and illuminates EUROPE! Tremble all ye oppressors of the world! Take warning all ye supporters of slavish governments and slavish hierarchies! Call no more (absurdly and wickedly) REFORMATION, innovation. You cannot now hold the world in darkness. Struggle no longer against increasing light and liberality. Restore to mankind their rights; and consent to the correction of abuses, before they and you are destroyed together.

10: *Second Report from the Committee of Secrecy Appointed by the House of Commons. Appendix C.*

Appendix C contained extracts from the Book of the Proceedings of the Society for Constitutional Information in London which had been seized after High Treason warrants had been issued against some of its members. The extract quoted was entered in the Book under the date, March 23, 1792, and was a copy of a letter which had been sent by a Sheffield Society trying to establish a "regular communication" with other Reform societies. The Report was ordered to be printed on June 6, 1794.

SHEFFIELD
14*th March*, 1792

SOCIETY FOR CONSTITUTIONAL INFORMATION

THIS Society, composed chiefly of the manufacturers of Sheffield, began about four months ago, and is already increased to nearly two thousand Members, and is daily increasing, exclusive of the adjacent towns and villages, who are forming themselves into similar Societies.

Considering, as we do, that the want of knowledge and information in the general mass of the People has exposed them to numberless impositions and abuses, the exertions of this Society are directed to the acquirement of useful knowledge, and to spread the same as far as our endeavours and abilities can extend.

We declare that we have derived more true knowledge from the two works of Mr. Thomas Paine, intituled *Rights of Man*, Part the First and Second, than from any other author or subject. The Practice as well as the principle of Government is laid down in those Works, in a manner so clear, and irresistibly convincing, that this Society do hereby resolve to give their Thanks to Mr. Paine for his two said publications . . . Also resolved unanimously, That the Thanks of this Society be given to Mr. Paine for the affectionate concern he has shewn in his Second Work in behalf of the poor, the infant, and the aged; who, notwithstanding the opulence which blesses other parts of the community, are by the grievous weight of taxes, rendered the miserable victims of poverty and wretchedness.

Resolved unanimously, That this Society, disdaining to be considered either of a ministerial or opposition party (names of which we are tired, having been so often deceived by both) do ardently recommend it to all their Fellow Citizens . . . to confer seriously and calmly with each other on the subject alluded to, and to manifest to the World that the spirit of true Liberty is a spirit of order; and that to obtain justice it is consistent that we be just ourselves.

Resolved unanimously, That these Resolutions be printed, and that a copy thereof be transmitted to the Society for Constitutional Information in London; requesting their approbation for twelve of our Friends to be entered into their Society, for the purpose of establishing a connection, and a regular communication with that, and all other similar Societies in the Kingdom.

11 : FROM *Mr. Paine's Letter to Mr. Secretary Dundas*, 1792

(Printed and Distributed by the Society for Constitutional Information in 12,000 copies)

LONDON
June 6, 1792

SIR,—As you opened the debate in the House of Commons, May 25th, on the Proclamation for suppressing Publications which that Proclamation . . . calls wicked and seditious, and as you applied those opprobrious epithets to the works entitled *Rights of Man* . . . I begin . . . by declaring, that I do not believe there are to be found in the writings of any author, ancient or modern, on the subject of Government, a spirit of greater benignity, and a stronger inculcation of moral principles than in those which I have published. They come, Sir, from a man who, by having lived in different countries and under different systems of Government and who, being intimate in the construction of them, is a better judge of the subject than it is possible that you, from the want of those opportunities, can be—and besides this, they come from a heart that knows not how to beguile . . .

In the First part of *Rights of Man*, I have endeavoured to show . . . that there does not exist a right to establish Hereditary Government . . . because Hereditary Government always means a Government yet to come, and the case always is, that the People who are to live afterwards, have always the same right

57

to chuse a government for themselves, as the People had who lived before them.

In the Second Part of *Rights of Man*, I have not repeated those arguments, because they are irrefutable; but have confined myself to show the defects of what is called Hereditary Government or Hereditary Succession . . . I do not know a greater good that an individual can render to mankind than to endeavour to break the chains of political superstition. Those chains are now dissolving fast, and proclamations and prosecutions will serve but to hasten that dissolution.

Having thus spoken of the Hereditary System as a bad system and subject to every possible defect, I now come to the Representative System . . . The system of Government purely representative, unmixed with any thing of hereditary nonsense, began in America . . . So powerful is the Representative System; first, by combining and consolidating all the parts of a country together, . . . and secondly, by admitting of none but men properly qualified into the Government or dismissing them if they prove to be otherwise, that America was enabled thereby totally to defeat and overthrow all the schemes and Projects of the Hereditary Government of England against her . . .

I now come to the comparative effects of the two systems *since* the close of the war . . . America had internally sustained the ravages of upwards of seven years of war, which England had not. England sustained only the expence of the war: whereas America sustained not only the expence, but the destruction of property committed by *both* armies . . . But such was the event, that the same Representative System of Government . . . though since better organised, which enabled her to conquer, enabled her also to recover; and she now presents a more flourishing condition, and a more happy and harmonised society . . . than any country in the world . . . Her towns are rebuilt much better than before: her commerce is spread all over the world . . .

I next come to state the expence of the two systems . . . The whole amount of the nett taxes in England . . . is seventeen millions . . . about nine millions is for the current annual expences . . . The expence of all the several departments of the General Representative Government of the United States, extending over a space nearly ten times larger than England . . . is £66,275 11s. sterling . . .

This is a Government that has nothing to fear. It needs no Proclamations to deter people from writing and reading. It needs no political superstition to support it. It was by encouraging discussion and rendering the press free . . . that the principles of Government became understood in America, and the people are now enjoying the present blessings under it. You hear of no riots, tumults, and disorders in that country . . .

In America there is not that class of poor and wretched people that are so numerously dispersed all over England, and who are to be told by a proclamation, that they are happy; and this is in a great measure to be accounted for, not by the difference of Proclamations, but by the difference of Governments and the difference of taxes . . . What the labouring people of that country earn, they apply to their own use, and to the education of their children, and do not pay it away in taxes, as fast as they earn it, to support Court extravagance, and a long enormous list of Placemen and Pensioners . . .

I have said in the Second Part of *Rights of Man*, and I repeat it here, that the service of any man, whether called King, President, Senator, Legislator, or any thing else, cannot be worth more to any country, in the regular routine of office, than Ten thousand pounds per annum . . . I have shown in the Second Part of *Rights of Man* that an alliance may be formed between England, France and America and that the expenses of Government in England may be put back to one million and a half . . . there will remain a surplus of nearly six million and a half out of the present Taxes, after paying the interest of the National Debt . . . and I have shown in the Second Part of *Rights of Man* what appears to be the best mode of applying the surplus money . . . to remit four millions . . . to the poor to be paid to them in money in proportion to the number of children in each family, and the number of aged persons . . .

12: REV. ROBERT HALL: *Apology for the Freedom of the Press and for General Liberty*, 1793

SINCE this pamphlet was first published, the principles it aims to support have received confirmation from such a train of disastrous events, that it might have been hoped we should have learned those lessons from misfortunes, which reason had failed to impress. Uninstructed by our calamities, we still persist in an impious attack on the liberties of France, and are eager to take our part in the great drama of crimes which is acting on the continent of Europe. Meantime the violence and injustice of the internal administration keeps pace with our iniquities abroad. Liberty and truth are silenced. An unrelenting system of persecution prevails. The cruel and humiliating sentences passed upon Mr. Muir and Mr. Palmer, men of unblemished morals and of the purest patriotism, the outrages committed on Dr. Priestley, and his intended removal to America, are events which will mark the latter end of the eighteenth century with indelible reproach. But what has liberty to expect from a minister, who has the audacity to assert the King's right to land as many foreign troops as he pleases, without the previous consent of Parliament? If this doctrine be true, the boasted equilibrium of the constitution, all the barriers which the wisdom of our ancestors have opposed to the encroachments of arbitrary power, are idle, ineffectual precautions . . . But it is needless any farther to expose the effrontery, or detect the sophistry, of this shameless apostate . . . A veteran in frauds while in the bloom of youth, betraying first, and then persecuting his earliest friends and connexions, falsifying every promise, and violating every political engagement, ever making the fairest professions a prelude to the darkest actions, punishing with the utmost rigour the publisher of the identical paper he himself had circulated, are traits in the conduct of Pitt, which entitle him to a fatal pre-eminence in guilt . . . Too long has he insulted the patience of his countrymen; nor ought we, when we observe the indifference with which the iniquities of Pitt's administration are viewed, to reproach the Romans for tamely submitting to the tyranny of Caligula or Domitian.

We had fondly hoped a mild philosophy was about to diffuse over the globe, the triumph of liberty and peace. But, alas! these hopes are fled. The continent presents little but one wide picture of desolation, misery and crimes . . .

That the seeds of public convulsions are sown in every country of Europe (our own not excepted) it were vain to deny, seeds which without the wisest precautions and the most conciliating councils, will break out, it is to be feared, in the overthrow of all governments. How this catastrophe may be averted . . . demands the deepest consideration of every European statesman. The ordinary routine of ministerial chicanery is quite unequal to the task. A philosophic comprehension of mind, which, leaving the beaten road of politics, shall adapt itself to new situations . . . these are the qualities which the situation of Europe renders indispensable. It would be a mockery of our present ministry to ask whether *they* possess those qualities . . .

(This passage is taken from the Advertisement to the Third Edition. Hall was a dissenting minister.)

13: *Second Report from the Committee of Secrecy appointed by the House of Lords.* Ordered to be printed June 7, 1794

In the course of the year 1793, a plan appears to have been conceived, and in some degree brought into a regular shape, for uniting the different meetings, formed by the artful dissemination of seditious publications, inviting men to follow the example of France, into such a body as might be brought to act to one given object, and be subject to one general direction.

The most marked effect of this plan was, the assembling of a body under the name of a Convention, which made its first public appearance at Edinburgh on the 29th of October 1793.

The design of this Meeting had been known and concerted for some time with Societies in England . . . After sitting four days in expectation of the English Delegates, the Meeting, which had consisted of about 150 persons from different parts of Scotland, separated, because the English Delegates had not arrived. In two days afterwards they came: a Delegate from Sheffield also arrived; and Sinclair . . . from the Society for Constitutional Information. Mr. Hamilton Rowan and Mr. Simon Butler, stating themselves to come on the part of a Society called the United Irishmen . . . made their appearance likewise . . .

A meeting of the Convention, which had separated before the appearance of these persons, was immediately summoned by Skirving the Secretary, and by public advertisement, for the 19th of November, on which day it was held, and consisted of about 160 persons.

The first four days of their Meeting were employed in settling forms, and in an examination of the Commissions of the Delegates supposed to be given by Meetings of the inhabitants of the places from which they were dated, but which Meetings were in very few places known to have existed, or to have been called for any such purpose. All these Commissions were of course allowed to be valid. On the 22nd day of November, this Meeting voted itself to be the British Convention, and assumed that style in their minutes and other proceedings, which were dated " in the first year of the British Convention " . . .

The Meeting thus formed, proceeded to act in exact imitation of the French Convention, adopting all its forms, phrases and modes of proceeding . . . and what may merit more serious attention than the affectation of this style, attempting to institute primary societies, provincial assemblies and departments in the country. On the 28th of November they came to a resolution of declared opposition and resistance to the authority of Parliament, under a reserve that it should not be entered on the minutes till the close of their sittings.

After this, the spirit and activity of the magistrates were exerted to disperse this Convention, and on the 5th of December 1793, the ringleaders were apprehended, their papers seized, and some of them have since been tried and convicted of the crimes laid to their charge . . .

From the time of the meeting and dispersion of the Convention at Edinburgh, the Societies in England began to act with increased vigour and activity. Their Resolutions expressed a warm approbation of the proceedings of the Convention at Edinburgh; strong declarations were made in behalf of those who had been brought to trial and convicted; subscriptions entered into for their encouragement and support; and some projects appear to have been entertained for their rescue . . .

The London Corresponding Society had continued to extend its correspondence, and also its influence with the other Societies dispersed in the Country, and had, in the month of February last, adopted a Resolution to arrange the Members into divisions of thirty, composed of those who lived nearest to each other, that they might easily be assembled together upon any emergency . . . besides the Section of Thirty, classed so as to be ready to come forth at the same time, there were to be secondary Sections of ten each . . . There was also a general Committee of Correspondence.

This Committee, in fact, appears to have existed for a considerable time, to have consisted of a number not exceeding Five, to have transacted and directed all the Secret Business of the Society, and they were authorised to communicate to the larger Meetings only such matters as they thought advisable . . .

Under this state of things . . . the project of procuring arms was brought forward. The precise date when it took place cannot be ascertained, for it appears to have been conducted in most places with peculiar secrecy and caution.

So early as the time of the Meeting at Edinburgh, the facility of procuring arms, particularly pikes, the use and efficacy of them as it had been proved in France, had been discussed at some of the Division Meetings; but no specific measure to this effect had been taken till a much later period.

About the month of March, 1794, private meetings had been held twice a week, in various places of and adjoining to the metropolis, for the purpose of instructing men in the use of the firelock; the places of such meeting were changed to avoid detection; and were chosen by a Committee . . . The number of fire-locks actually provided . . . may seem inconsiderable for the execution of any design . . . but . . . it appears that the Artillery House, and gunsmith shops in various parts of the metropolis were looked to as furnishing a ready resource . . .

The use of pikes formed a still more considerable part of the intended armament. The effect of this weapon had often been discussed at Meetings, and a correspondence had been entered into with persons at Sheffield for providing a supply of them . . .

On the most deliberate consideration of all the evidence there are the most convincing proofs, not only of a plan formed in theory, to procure, by legal means, some partial change of the laws . . . but of a formed conspiracy to assemble, under the name of a convention, a number of persons assuming to be the Representatives of the Nation, for the express purpose of making their Resolutions to be Law, and of subverting, by their authority, the whole frame of the Government, and the Constitution of this realm . . .

The Committee must farther observe, that there is also as strong a degree of evidence as the nature of the case will admit, that the aim of the leaders in this Conspiracy extended to as complete a Revolution in this country as that which has taken place in France since the month of August 1792 . . .

14: *Account of the Proceedings of a Meeting of the London Corresponding Society held in a Field near Copenhagen House, Monday October 26, 1795 . . . and the Resolutions passed by upwards of Two Hundred Thousand Citizens, then and there assembled, 1795*

ADDRESS TO THE NATION
(ADOPTED BY THE MEETING)

WITH anxious minds and agitated hearts we are again compelled to address you . . . Four months ago we peaceably assembled to deliberate upon the best and most probable mode of recovering our rights, and redressing our numerous grievances . . . We believe, if we may judge from the rapid increase of our numbers since our last public meeting, that our sentiments and conduct experienced almost general approbation . . .

To delineate a faithful portrait of the awful situation of our distracted country, would only be to exhibit a scene of misery and desolation . . . The history of the last few months presents indeed to our view, a rapid succession of ill-fated mismanagement, unexampled calamities and unparalleled disgrace! Baffled and defeated in every miserable project they have either designed or undertaken, Ministers seem determined to display their pre-eminent power of doing mischief : and as they cannot compass the ruin of France, to contrive at least the destruction of England! Emigrant Armies and Foreign Expeditions have been hastily planned and equipped, to ensure only to the one, a horrible and undistinguished carnage ; and to the other a premature and untimely grave! . . . The bread that should support the industrious poor has been exported, either to be abandoned on a foreign shore, or consigned to the bottom . . .

The comfortable and pleasing prospects resulting from an abundant harvest have turned out to be vain and fallacious . . . and were probably held up only to lull the public mind . . . the approach of famine seems to be inevitable . . .

What is the evil and insatiate monster that thus piecemeal turns and devours us? . . . Why, when we incessantly toil and labour, must we pine in misery and want? What is this subtle and insinuating poison which

... destroys our public prosperity? It is *Parliamentary Corruption.*

... We are sincere friends of Peace—we want only Reform—a thorough Reform—but we cannot answer for the strong and all-powerful impulse of necessity nor always restrain the aggravated feeling of insulted human nature!

15: *Report of the Committee of Secrecy of the House of Commons.* Ordered to be printed March 15, 1799

AT the meetings of the London Corresponding Society, for above two years before this time (1798), it had been avowed that the object of the Society was to form a republic, by the assistance of France. Reform in Parliament, or even annual elections, or universal suffrage, were therefore no longer mentioned . . . Meetings were held, to contrive the means of procuring arms, to enable them to co-operate with a French force in the case of invasion . . . The leading members of the disaffected societies were also in the habit of frequenting an occasional meeting, which was held at a cellar in Furnivall's Inn, and was first formed for the purpose of reading the libellous and treasonable publication, called the *Press*. It was particularly attended by Arthur O'Connor and O'Coigly . . . and by the persons chiefly instrumental in carrying on correspondence with the Irish conspirators; and secret consultations were repeatedly held there, with a view to projects, which were thought to be too dangerous and desperate to be brought forward in any of the larger societies. Among these plans was that of effecting a general insurrection, at the same moment, in the metropolis, and throughout the country, and of directing it to the object of seizing or assassinating the king, the royal family, and many members of both houses of parliament . . .

Attempts were, at the same time, made to form, in London, upon the plan of the United Irishmen, the Society of United Englishmen, or United Britons . . . Most of the societies through England, which had used to correspond with the London Corresponding Society, had also about this time adopted the same plan of forming societies of United Englishmen . . .

Information having been received of a meeting of United Englishmen, to be held at a house in Clerken-well, warrants of arrest were issued, and persons were apprehended on the 18th of April 1798 . . . Information having also been received of an extraordinary meeting of the delegates and secretary of the London Corresponding Society, . . . on the 19th of April 1798, the persons there assembled were likewise arrested . . .

It appeared, that about forty divisions of United Englishmen had been formed in London; about twenty of which had their regular places and days of meeting; and that many similar societies were forming in different parts of the country . . . At Manchester, and in the adjacent country in particular, the plan of these conspiracies was extending itself in the most alarming manner . . . A society of United Englishmen had been established in and about Manchester before the year 1797. In the beginning of that year it consisted of about fifty divisions, and in the year 1798 had extended to about eighty . . . This society had been particularly active in the most wicked attempts to seduce the soldiers . . . It frequently sent delegates . . . Liverpool also became the seat of another central society . . .

16: Sir Francis Burdett: Speech at Brentford, November 10, 1806 (*Cobbett's Weekly Political Register*, November 15, 1806):

" Gentlemen, Mr. Whitbread tells us in his Manifesto, that the Administration of which he is so conspicuous a supporter have not yet formed their *projected schemes of reform, internal and external.* Thus it appears, that they have their schemes in agitation. Now what is the absurd outcry raised against me? That I am a schemer. That I have dangerous schemes which I wish to execute. Believe me, Gentlemen, and it is the sacred assurance of an honest, independent, and, I trust, virtuous man, I have no schemes; I meditate no innovations; I want nothing but the constitution of England, my beloved country; I want the whole of that constitution, and nothing but that constitution ".

17: Sir Francis Burdett: *Address to the Electors of Westminster, after the Election* (May 23, 1807):

" Gentlemen, next to the consciousness of endeavouring sincerely to serve my country, nothing can be more pleasing to my mind than the public approbation of my endeavours. Accept my grateful thanks. At the same time forgive me for feeling something like despair of any good to the country . . . Such is my conception of the different corrupt ministers we have seen, and their corrupt adherents. And unless the public with an united voice, shall loudly pronounce the abolition of the whole of the present SYSTEM OF CORRUPTION, I must still continue to despair of my country. You, Gentlemen, by this unparalleled election, have loudly pronounced your sentiments. May your voice be echoed through the land . . . And I assure you that no rational endeavours of mine shall be omitted to restore to my countrymen the undisturbed enjoyment of the fair fruits of their industry; to tear out the accursed leaves of that scandalous RED BOOK (of pensions and sinecures); and to bring back men's minds to the almost forgotten notions of the sacredness of private property; which ought no longer to be transferred from the legitimate possessors by the corrupt votes of venal and mercenary combinations . . .

18: *A Full and Accurate Report of the Proceedings at the Meeting held at the Crown and Anchor Tavern, on Monday, the 1st of May, 1809 relative to a Reform in the Commons House of Parliament*

MAJOR Cartwright rose, and . . . read the Resolutions one by one, amidst the reiterated acclamations of the crowded audience.

Resolved, 1. That it is the grand principle of the Constitution, that the People shall have a share in the Government, by a just representation in Parliament.

2. That the long duration of Parliaments greatly facilitates the corruption of the members, and removes that wholesome check or controul on their conduct— a frequent recurrence to the opinion of their Constituents.

3. That in a Petition, presented to the House of Commons on the 6th of May, 1793, it was offered to be proved at the Bar, "that 154 individuals did, by their own authority, appoint or procure the return of

307 Members of that House . . . who were thus enabled to decide all questions in the name of the whole People of Great Britain ".

4. That this Meeting believes that individual patronage in Boroughs has increased since 1793—that the Representation of Scotland is extremely influenced and unfree—that there are great defects in that of Ireland—and that in the English Boroughs called OPEN, the returns are for the most part obtained for money . . .

5. That in the Act (commonly called the Act of Settlement) . . . it was asserted, and recognised as a Constitutional principle, that no person who " has an office of place or profit under the King, or receives a pension from the Crown, shall be capable of serving as a Member of the House of Commons ".

6. That it appears, by a Report laid on the table of the House of Commons in June last, that 78 of its Members are in the regular receipt under the Crown of £178,994 a year.

7. That in 1782, it was declared by Mr. Pitt in the House of Commons that " seven or eight members of that House were sent there by the Nabob of Arcot, and that a foreign state in enmity to this country might procure a party to act for it under the mask and character of Members of that House ".

8. That such a state of Representation is a national grievance.

9. That in every department of the State, into which inquiry has been made, scandalous corruptions and abuses have been detected.

10. That the exclusion of the public voice from all influence in, and the consequent corruption of, the Governments of the Continental States, have been the causes of their subjugation.

11. That so long as the People shall not be fairly represented, corruption will increase; our debts and taxes will accumulate; our resources will be dissipated; the native energy of the People will be depressed; and the country deprived of its best defence against foreign foes.

12. That to remedy the great and glaring evils of which we complain, it is not necessary to have recourse to theoretical speculations or dangerous experiments in Government, but to recur to the principles handed down to us by the wisdom and virtue of our forefathers.

13. That the remedy is to be found, and to be found only, in a full and fair Representation of the People in the Commons House of Parliament . . .

14. That we therefore recommend to every town, city, and county, to take the state of the Representation into consideration, and urgently, but temperately, to apply to Parliament . . .

19: The City of London's Petition to the House of Commons, adopted May 4, 1810

We, the Lord Mayor, Aldermen, and Livery of the City of London, in Common Hall assembled, beg leave, with feelings of the most anxious concern, to present this our humble Address, Petition, and Remonstrance . . .

The circumstance which most deeply afflicts us . . . is . . . you have imprisoned two of your fellow-subjects, and that, without a trial, without a hearing, you have condemned them . . . Mr. John Gale Jones and Sir Francis Burdett . . .

Permit us humbly to observe, that the construction of your Hon. House prevents our surprize at this conduct . . . upwards of 300 Members of your Hon. House, in England and Wales only, are not elected by the People . . . but are sent to your Hon. House by the absolute nomination or powerful influence of about 150 Peers and others . . . This is the great constitutional disease of our country. This is the true root of all evils, corruptions, and oppressions, under which we labour. If it be not eradicated, the nation must perish.

In support of this our sincere conviction, we need only refer to the never-to-be-forgotten vote of your Hon. House, refusing to examine evidence on a charge against Lord Castlereagh and Mr. Perceval, then two of the King's Ministers, for trafficking in seats in your Hon. House . . .

Lord Castlereagh continued to be a principal Minister . . . Sir Francis Burdett, dragged by a military force from the bosom of his family, is committed to the Tower for exercising the right of constitutional discussion—Mr. Spencer Perceval continues—the chief adviser of the Royal Councils.

Under the agonizing feelings excited by the late imprisonment of our fellow-subjects, can it be necessary for us to recapitulate the many instances . . . of refusals to institute just and necessary inquiry, to pursue to condign punishment public delinquents and peculators, to economize the means and resources of the State, to administer to the people relief and redress for the various disgraces which the national honour has sustained, for the lavish profusion of British blood and treasure, extravagantly wasted in ill-contrived and fruitless campaigns, and more particularly in the humiliating and ignominious expedition to the Coast of Holland, in which the greatest armament that ever left our shores, was exposed to the scorn, contempt, and ridicule of the enemy; and the flower of the British Army left ingloriously to perish in the pestilential marshes of Walcheren, without succour! without necessity! without object! without hope! . . .

We therefore humbly, but firmly, entreat you to reconsider your conduct . . .

Above all we earnestly pray your Honourable House, in conjunction with Sir Francis Burdett, and in conformity to the notice he has given, to devise and adopt such measures as will effect an immediate and radical Reform in the Commons House of Parliament, and to insure to the People a full, fair, and substantial Representation . . .

(From *Blagdon's Political Register*, May 9, 1810)

20 : ADDRESS AND PETITION OF THE COMMON COUNCIL OF THE CITY OF LONDON, April 28, 1812. (New Annual Register)

THE right hon. the lord mayor, aldermen, sheriffs, and common council of the city of London waited upon his royal highness the prince regent . . . with the following address and petition . . .

" May it please your royal highness, We, the lord mayor, aldermen, and commons of the City of London . . . humbly approach your royal highness, dutifully to represent . . . the difficulties and dangers impending over the country, and anxiously to invite your beneficent attention to the complaints and grievances of your afflicted but faithful subjects. Fourteen months have elapsed since your royal highness acceded to the

75

regency . . . at which time we felt it our duty to submit to you a statement of the abuses which had taken root in the various departments of the government, the speedy correction and removal of which we deemed essential to the prosperity and safety of the empire; and we now again present ourselves . . . to express our unfeigned sorrow, that during this interval no efficient measures have been adopted by your ministers . . . but that, on the contrary, the same mal-practices, and the same false principles of government, have been tenaciously pursued and enforced . . . We have continued to witness the same system of profligacy in the expenditure of the public money; the same system of governing by undue influence and corruption; the same system of delusion in regard to the circulating medium and finances of the country; the same system of arbitrary and grievous assessment and collection of taxes . . . ; the same system of introducing into the heart of the country foreign troops; the same system of persecuting the press . . . and, finally, the same system of coercive restrictions on the freedom of commerce, by which many of our merchants and manufacturers have been involved in ruin . . . As faithful and loyal subjects . . . we feel the deepest affliction in being thus compelled to reiterate this enumeration of the mal-practices and mistaken principles of, your ministers . . . your confidential advisers have plunged this great and once flourishing empire into an abyss, from which we can be rescued only by radical reforms . . . We therefore pray, that your royal highness will be graciously pleased to dismiss from your councils those ministers who have proved themselves so undeserving of the confidence of your people, and call to the administration of the government men of public character and patriotic principles, whose enlarged and liberal policy is suited to the enlightened character of the nation . . . and whose public spirit would stimulate them to effect those reforms in the commons house of parliament, and in the various branches of the state, which at this perilous crisis are absolutely necessary to the restoration of national prosperity . . .

21 : JOHN FOSTER: Letter of June 30, 1812

YOU are at Cobbett again . . . you talk of his "truths not less dangerous than his falsehoods"; which is just the kind of lingo with which people are . . . perplexed, frightened and gulled into an acquiescence with all the corruptions and mischiefs of the political state and course of things, while he is plainly and boldly enforcing a few great obvious principles, and illustrating them by a perpetual reference to facts. *He* was plainly stating and predicting, all along, how our management as to America *must* operate: behold the consequence of despising all he said. *He* has all along urged the necessity of concession to the Catholics, and the abolition of flogging; he was a " pestilent sower of sedition ", as you say, for his pains; but how odd it is that the whole State is coming round to him so fast! *He* predicted the whole process of the paper-money, and warned against augmenting the evil; it was all seditious and *false*, for it has been substantially fulfilled. *He* has constantly represented that a Parliament constituted like ours will scorn all checks on the waste of public money;—seditious and false, as witness the whole system of our outgoings, and not last nor least, the vast and increasing account of sinecures and pensions. And twenty more such things: all " dangerous falsehoods "

—or are these exposures " the dangerous, the equally
dangerous *truths* . . ."? Only it amazes one that
Cobbett's dubious morality, and his being erroneous,
perhaps, now and then in minor points . . . should really
have the effect to turn so much urgent and awful truth
into such comfortable falsehood that the nation may
sleep quite at its ease . . .

(*Life and Correspondence of John Foster*, 1846. Letter
of June 30, 1812)

22 : THE WESTMINSTER PETITION AGAINST THE CORN
LAW OF 1815. (*Hansard's Parliamentary
Debates*, VOL. XXX)

" . . . on the unexpected and fortunate return of peace
it was reasonable to hope . . . that the rent of land and
the prices of provisions would be reduced; that some
of the more grievous and burthensome taxes would
cease; that commerce would flow into its accustomed
channels; that a stimulus would be given to our
manufacturing and trading interests by the freedom
of intercourse with foreign nations; and that all classes
of our fellow-subjects would participate in those
blessings and advantages to which they had formerly
been accustomed in times of tranquillity.

" That your petitioners have, however, noticed with
extreme concern and anxiety the introduction into your
honourable House of a Bill relative to the importation
of corn, which if passed into a law, must necessarily
and directly produce, and, in the judgement of your
petitioners, is intended to produce, a great permanent
increase in the price of one of the first necessaries of
life, for the sake of enabling the proprietors and

cultivators of land to maintain undiminished a splendid
and luxurious style of living, unknown to their fathers,
in which they were tempted to indulge during the late
war, so highly profitable to them, and so calamitous to
their fellow-subjects ".

Part III

FROM WATERLOO TO THE
REFORM BILL

1815–1832

FROM WATERLOO TO THE
REFORM BILL

1815–1832

ENGLISH industry and agriculture had, during the long war-years between 1793 and 1815, become so based on war conditions that the return of peace produced the greatest economic dislocation. The dislocation was the worse from the fact that not the slightest administrative preparation or study had been made of the problems which peace would bring. The years, therefore, between 1816 and 1821, which would in any case have been transition-years of exceptional difficulty, proved to be a period of great calamity for the poor, who were gravely affected by declining employment and falling wages. Once again a cry arose for a Parliament that would really give the masses the representation which they needed. The agitation was led by Cobbett in the Press and by Orator Hunt on the demagogic platform. No. 23 gives an idea of the power of Cobbett's writing, eagerly read by the poor in the twopenny reprints from *Cobbett's Weekly Register*, dubbed by his opponents as " Twopenny Trash ". Nos. 24 and 25 were written by Samuel Bamford, a Lancashire silk-weaver twice arrested on suspicion of high treason, to explain to the Chartists over twenty years afterwards what avoidable mistakes they were repeating despite the experience of his own generation. No. 25, extracted from Bamford's *Passages in the Life of a Radical*, gives a specially interesting picture of " Peterloo ", as seen through the eyes of one of the principal organisers of the great Radical gathering at St. Peter's Fields, Manchester, on August 16, 1819.

The politics of 1821 and 1822 are mirrored, to some extent, in Document No. 26,[1] with its account of motions on Peterloo, Repeal of the Six Acts, Army Reductions, Tax and Expenditure Reductions, Sinecure Reductions, Irish Tithe Reform, and, of course, Parliamentary Reform. It is true that the Liberal Tories, helped by the end of post-war depression, undertook some important reforms between 1823 and 1827 which earned the praise even of the Philosophical Radicals, the important new group forming round Bentham and James Mill and already possessed of some influence.[2] It is true also that both in 1828 and 1829 the Duke of Wellington's Government was forced by the " spirit of the age " to continue in the path of concession until the Duke split his own party by conceding Catholic Emancipation in 1829, and failed to re-unite it in 1830 by refusing to yield in the slightest on Parliamentary Reform. Yet when the Wellington Government fell in November 1830 and was succeeded by the administration of Lord Grey, pledged to the cause of Reform, John Wade, author of the original *Black Book*, issued a new edition of what was already known as the " Reformer's Bible ", in order to show the tremendous mass of abuse that needed to be dealt with and the great danger that the Cabinet would attempt only a

[1] This document is extracted from the Supplement, issued in 1823, to that remarkable account of official nepotism, venality and selfishness, which was published in 1820 as the *Black Book* and speedily adopted as the popular text-book of abuses.

[2] But see No. 27 for the doubts of one acute Radical Dissenter, who questioned the wisdom of the support given in 1827 to Canning in the hope of attaining Catholic Emancipation with his aid.

patchwork compromise even on Parliamentary Reform, the necessary preliminary to all the rest.

Wade's call to the people (No. 28), in the *Extraordinary Black Book* of 1831, for "watchfulness" and "demonstrations" proved to be amply justified before "the Bill, the whole Bill and nothing but the Bill" was put on the Statute Book in 1832. No. 29 is an account of the greatest demonstration organised in 1832 by the Political Unions,the radical associations formed in many places to make sure that a far-reaching Parliamentary Reform was placed upon the Statute Book in spite of the House of Lords and other hostile influences. The Reform Bill, though saved practically entire by such demonstrations, was widely regarded as a mere beginning of the changes that would have to be undertaken. Among those who had the largest ideas of the improvements that would become possible were the Philosophical Radicals, small but influential groups of whom, looking to James Mill and Bentham for inspiration, had already begun their important permeation of the thinking of the governing classes. It was James Mill's *Essay on Government* (parts of which are quoted in No. 30), which represented one of the moving forces of "Philosophic" or "Intellectual Radicalism" both before and after the Reform Bill. In the *Essay* will be found such epoch-making phrases as "the greatest happiness of the greatest number", borrowed from Bentham and widely popularised as the main end of Government; the almost equally historic phrase, "the whole product of Labour" as Labour's due; and, finally, an interesting adaptation of the Social Contract theory, leading up to the most "scientific" case yet made out for Short Parliaments and virtually Universal Suffrage for male adults.

Bentham had already demanded a Radical Reform Bill in some vigorous pamphleteering of 1817, but the portion of Bentham's writing chosen for reproduction in No. 31 is not this but extracts from a sixpenny pamphlet, issued in 1831 from the office of the Philosophical Radicals' *Westminster Review*, and embodying Bentham's ideas, as laid down in his *Constitutional Code*, on the proper declaration of principles to be expected from Parliamentary candidates. The anti-Imperialism, the anti-Colonialism and the anti-Militarism, inculcated by Bentham, became characteristic of much later Radical thought.

23: WILLIAM COBBETT: *Weekly Political Register,*
Saturday, November 2, 1816. (Vol. 31, No. 3)

To the Journeymen and Labourers of England, Wales, Scotland, and Ireland, on the Cause of their present Miseries ...

FRIENDS AND FELLOW-COUNTRYMEN,

Whatever the Pride of rank, of riches or of scholarship, may have induced some men to believe, or to affect to believe, the real strength and all the resources of a country, ever have sprung and ever must spring, from the *labour* of its people; and hence it is, that this nation, which is so small in numbers and so poor in climate and soil compared with many others, has, for many ages, been the most powerful nation in the world: it is the most industrious, the most laborious, and, therefore, the most powerful. Elegant dresses, superb furniture, stately buildings, fine roads and canals, fleet horses and carriages, numerous and stout ships, warehouses teeming with goods ... all these spring from *labour*. Without the Journeyman and the labourer none of them could exist . . .

As it is the labour of those who toil which makes a country abound in resources, so it is the same class of men, who must, by their arms, secure its safety and uphold its fame. Titles and immense sums of money have been bestowed upon numerous Naval and Military Commanders. Without calling the justice of these in question, we may assert that the victories were obtained by *you* and your fathers and brothers and sons in co-operation with those Commanders, who, with *your* aid have done great and wonderful things; but, who, without that aid, would have been as impotent as children at the breast.

With this correct idea of your own worth in your minds, with what indignation must you hear yourselves called the Populace, the Rabble, the Mob, the Swinish Multitude; and with what greater indignation, if possible, must you hear the projects of those cool and cruel and insolent men, who, now that you have been, without any fault of yours, brought into a state of misery, propose to narrow the limits of parish relief, to prevent you from marrying in the days of your youth, or to thrust you out to seek your bread in foreign lands . . .

As to the cause of our present miseries, it is the *enormous amount of the taxes,* which the government compels us to pay for the support of its army, its place-men, its pensioners, &c. and for the payment of the interest of its debt . . . Indeed, when we compare our present state to the state of the country previous to the wars against France, we must see that our present misery is owing to no other cause. The taxes then annually raised amounted to about 15 millions: they amounted last year to 70 millions. The nation was then happy: it is now miserable ... We next come to consider, what have been *the causes of this weight of taxes.* Here we must go back a little in our history, and you will soon see, that this intolerable weight has *all proceeded from the want of a Parliamentary Reform.*

In the year 1764, soon after the present king came to the throne, the annual interest of the debt amounted to about five millions, and the whole of the taxes to about nine millions. But, soon after this a war was entered on to compel the Americans to submit to be taxed by the Parliament, *without being represented in that Parliament.* The Americans triumphed, and, after the war was over, the annual interest of the Debt amounted to about nine millions, and the whole of the taxes to about 15 millions. This was our situation, when the French people began their Revolution. The French people had so long been the slaves of a despotic government, that the friends of freedom in England rejoiced at their emancipation. The cause of *reform,* which had never ceased to have supporters in England for a great many years, now acquired a new life, and the Reformers urged the Parliament to *grant reform* instead of going to war against the people of France ... The Parliament, instead of listening to the Reformers, *crushed them,* and went to war against the people of France: and the consequence of these wars is, that the annual interest of the Debt now amounts to 45 millions, and the whole of the taxes, during each of the last several years, to 70 millions ...

Seeing that the *cause* of your misery is the *weight of taxation,* one would expect to hear of nothing but a *reduction of taxation* in the way of remedy; but from the friends of corruption, never we do hear of any such remedy. To hear them, one would think that *you* had been the guilty cause of the misery you suffer, and you alone ought to be made answerable for what has taken place. The emissaries of corruption are now continually crying out against the *weight* of the *poor-rates* . . . Their project is to deny relief to all who are *able to work*. But what is the use of your being able to work, if no one will, or can, give you work? . . . The notion of these people seems to be, that every body that receives money out of the taxes have a *right* to receive it, except *you* . . .

But the complaints of these persons against you are the more unreasonable, because they say not a word against the sums paid to *Sinecure Placemen* and *Pensioners* . . . There are of these places and pensions all sizes from *twenty pounds* to *thirty thousand* and nearly *forty thousand pounds a year*! And, surely, these ought to be done away before any proposition be made to take the parish allowance from any of you, who are unable to work, or to find work to do. There are several individual placemen, the profits of each of which would maintain *a thousand families*. The names of the *Ladies* upon the pension list would, if printed one under another, fill a sheet of paper like this . . .

You have been represented by *The Times* newspaper, by the *Courier*, by the *Morning Post* . . . as the *Scum* of Society. They say, that you have *no business at public meetings*; that you are *rabble*, and that you *pay no taxes*. These insolent hirelings, who wallow in wealth, would not be able to put their abuse of you in print were it not for *your labour*. You create all that is an object of taxation; for even the *land* itself would be good for nothing without your labour. But are you *not taxed*? Do you pay *no taxes*? . . . The *tax-*

gatherers do not, indeed, come to *you* and demand money of you: but there are few articles which you use, in the purchase of which you do not pay a *tax*. On your Shoes, Salt, Beer, Malt, Hops, Tea, Sugar, Candles, Soap, Paper, Coffee, Spirits, Glass of your Windows, Bricks and Tiles, Tobacco, on all these, and many other articles you pay a *tax* . . . In several cases the tax amounts to more than one half of what you pay for the article itself . . . and the ruffians of the hired press call you the *Scum* of society, and deny that you have the right to show your faces at any public meeting to petition for a reform, or for the removal of any abuse whatever . . .

24: SAMUEL BAMFORD: *Passages in the Life of a Radical*. This extract was written about 1840. (From Chapter 2)

IT is a matter of history, that whilst the laurels were yet cool on the brows of our victorious soldiers on their second occupation of Paris, the elements of convulsion were at work amongst the masses of our labouring population; and that a series of disturbances commenced with the introduction of the Corn Bill in 1815, and continued, with short intervals, until the close of the year 1816. In London and Westminster riots ensued, and were continued for several days, whilst the Bill was discussed; at Bridport, there were riots on account of the high price of bread; at Bideford there were similar disturbances to prevent the exportation of grain; at Bury, by the unemployed, to destroy machinery; at Ely, not suppressed without bloodshed; at Newcastle-on-Tyne, by colliers and others; at

Glasgow, where blood was shed, on account of the soup kitchens; at Preston, by unemployed weavers; at Nottingham, by Luddites, who destroyed thirty frames; at Merthyr Tydville, on a reduction of wages; at Birmingham, by the unemployed; at Walsall, by the distressed; and December 7th, 1816, at Dundee, where owing to the high price of meal, upwards of one hundred shops were plundered. At this time the writings of William Cobbett suddenly became of great authority; they were read on nearly every cottage hearth in the manufacturing districts of South Lancashire, in those of Leicester, Derby, and Nottingham; also in many of the Scottish manufacturing towns . . .

Instead of riots and destruction of property, Hampden clubs were now established in many of our large towns, and the villages and districts around them; Cobbett's books were printed in a cheap form; the labourers read them, and thenceforward became deliberate and systematic in their proceedings. Nor were there wanting men of their own class, to encourage and direct the new converts; the Sunday Schools of the previous thirty years, had produced many working men of sufficient talents to become readers, writers, and speakers in the village meetings for parliamentary reform . . .

One of these clubs was established in 1816, at the small town of Middleton, near Manchester; and I, having been instrumental in its formation, a tolerable reader also, and a rather expert writer, was chosen secretary. The club prospered; the number of members increased; the funds raised by contributions of a penny a week became more than sufficient . . . and taking a bold step, we soon rented a chapel which had been given up by a society of Kilhamite Methodists. This place we threw open for the religious worship of all sects and parties, and there we held our meetings on the evenings of Monday and Saturday in each week . . .

Several meetings of delegates from the surrounding districts were held at our chapel on which occasions the leading reformers of Lancashire were generally seen together . . . One of our delegate meetings deserves particular notice. It was held on Sunday, the 16th December 1816; when it was determined to send out missionaries, to other towns and villages, particularly to Yorkshire . . .

On the first of January, 1817, a meeting of delegates from twenty-one petitioning bodies, was held in our chapel, when resolutions were passed declaratory of the right of every male to vote, who paid taxes; that males of eighteen should be eligible to vote; that parliaments should be elected annually; that no placeman or pensioner should sit in parliament; that every twenty thousand inhabitants should send a member to the house of commons; and that talent, and virtue, were the only qualifications necessary . . .

25: EXTRACTS FROM SAMUEL BAMFORD: *Passages in the Life of a Radical*

AMONGST the meetings for reform held in the early part of the summer of 1819, were the one which took place on Spafields, London, at which Mr. Hunt was chairman; and another held at Birmingham, at which Major Cartwright and Sir Charles Wolseley were elected to act as legislatorial attornies for that town in Parliament.

It would seem that these movements in the country,

induced our friends at Manchester to adopt a course similar to that at Birmingham . . . and it was accordingly arranged that a meeting for that purpose should be held on St. Peter's Field . . .

By eight o'clock on the morning of Monday, the 16th of August 1819, the whole town of Middleton might be said to be on the alert; some to go to the meeting, and others to see the procession; the like of which for such a purpose, had never before taken place, in that neighbourhood.

First were selected twelve of the most comely and decent-looking youths . . . with each a branch of laurel held presented in his hand, as a token of amity and peace, then followed the men of several districts in fives, then the band of music, an excellent one, then the colours; a blue one of silk, with inscriptions in golden letters, " UNITY AND STRENGTH ", " LIBERTY AND FRATERNITY "; green one of silk, with golden letters, " PARLIAMENTS ANNUAL ", " SUFFRAGE UNIVERSAL "; and betwixt them on a staff, a handsome cap of crimson velvet, with a tuft of laurel, and the cap tastefully braided with the word, LIBERTAS, in front. Next were placed the remainder of the men of the districts in fives . . .

Our whole column, with the Rochdale people, would probably consist of six thousand men. At our head were a hundred or two of women, mostly young wives, and mine was amongst them. A hundred or two of our handsomest girls—sweethearts to the lads who were with us—danced to the music, or sung snatches of popular songs . . . whilst on each side of our line walked some thousands of stragglers . . .

At Blackley, the accession to our ranks, and the crowd in the road had become much greater. At

Harpurhey, we halted . . . At Newtown we were welcomed with open arms by the poor Irish weavers . . . We learned that other parties were on the field before us, and that the Lees and Saddleworth Union had been led by Doctor Healey, walking before a pitch-black flag, with staring white letters, forming the words, " EQUAL REPRESENTATION OR DEATH ", " LOVE ", two hands joined, and a heart . . .

Successive parties kept arriving on the ground, and we became deeper enclosed, until we occupied about the centre of that vast multitude . . . In about half an hour after our arrival at the meeting, the sounds of music, and reiterated shouts, proclaimed the near approach of Mr. Hunt and his party . . . He mounted the hustings; the music ceased; Mr. Johnson proposed that Mr. Hunt should take the chair; it was seconded and carried by acclamation; and Mr. Hunt, stepping towards the front of the stage, took off his white hat, and addressed the people . . . a noise and strange murmur arose towards the church . . .

On the cavalry drawing up they were received with a shout, of good will, as I understood it. They shouted again, waving their sabres over their heads; and then, slackening rein, and striking spur into their steeds, they dashed forward, and began cutting the people . . .

In ten minutes from the commencement of the havock, the field was an open and almost deserted space . . . The hustings remained, with a few broken and hewed flagstaves erect, and a torn and gashed banner or two dropping; whilst over the whole field, were strewed caps, bonnets, hats, shawls, and shoes, and other parts of male and female dress; trampled, torn, and bloody. The yeomanry had dismounted,—some were easing their horses' girths, others adjusting their accoutrements; and some were wiping their sabres. Several mounds of human beings still remained where they had fallen, crushed down and smothered. Some of these still groaning, others with staring eyes, were gasping for breath, and others would never breathe more.

(This description of Peterloo is taken from Chapters 30–35.)

26: JOHN WADE: *The Black Book,* VOL. 2, *or Corruption Unmasked,* 1823

From the Introduction.
THERE are two ways by which the condition of a country may be ameliorated, and its happiness and greatness augmented: first, the policy of government may directly contribute to that end, or, secondly, the people, by their own energies, may work out an improvement in their situation. England has been placed in the latter predicament, her improvements have all originated with the People; it is to the People that every increase in liberty, intellect, or wealth may be traced.

This judgement is warranted by history. It is hardly possible to fix on any period, under any minister, when the spirit of improvement was fostered by government, when men of genius were patronized, or when any anxiety was manifested to facilitate the operations of industry, by abstaining from burdening it with imposts. On the contrary, history exhibits only the virtues of the People struggling against the vices of power,—of liberty against oppression,—of industry against the rapacity of taxation,—of truth against established error. Nevertheless, in spite of these obstacles the country has continued to flourish; but its prosperity . . . is not to be dated from the Revolution, nor the reign of George III, nor the Pitt System, nor any other system; neither is it the work of any faction, Whig or Tory; nor of any dynasty either of the Tudor, the Stuart, or the Hanoverian race. No; it is to none of these causes; it is to the People themselves . . .

Five things at least might have been expected from an enlightened administration: — First, a general system for the education of the People, founded, not on any system of religious exclusion, or political injustice, but on the basis of Truth. Secondly, a provision for the clergy, independently of tithe, which is so oppressive on agriculture, and adapted only to a different state of society. Thirdly, a more simple and economical mode of taxation, embracing an abolition of such internal duties as, without adding proportionately to public revenue, interfere with the operations of commercial and manufacturing industry. Fourthly, a revision of the civil and criminal jurisprudence. Lastly, as a necessary preliminary to the rest, an extension of the basis of representation, so as to embrace the intellect, virtue, and property of the community.

These ameliorations might have been all quietly effected within the last century. Instead, however, of government being occupied on these truly national objects, it has been a mere arena for aristocratical contention, on which these pseudo patriots—these "Great Men" as they are sometimes called, the Godolphins, the Somers, the Harleys, the Bolingbrokes, the Chathams, Foxes, Burkes, and Pitts, have displayed their selfishness and ambition . . .

From the BLACK BOOK'S *" Key to the Lower House,
Showing the most important Questions on which the
Members have voted . . . the Offices, Pensions, Grants,
Church-Preferment, or other Emolument enjoyed by
themselves or families . . ."*

When a Member is said to have voted for *Parliamentary Reform*, it is meant he voted for Lord John
Russell's motion on that subject, on the 25th of April
(1822): it was the only motion on Reform last session;
it did not embrace any principle, and was merely
declaratory, " That the present state of the representation of the People in Parliament required the serious
consideration of that House." It was an important
question, from the great number of members that
voted; and from distinguishing those who are in favour
of Reform of *some kind* from those opposed to *all*
Reform. The large minority of 164 on the occasion,
shows the progress Reform is making in the most
unfavourable soil. When a Member is said to have
voted *against* the influence of the Crown, it is meant
he voted for Mr. Brougham's motion on that subject,
on the 24th of June. Mr. Brougham's motion was,
" That the influence now possessed by the Crown
is unnecessary for maintaining its constitutional
prerogatives, destructive of the independence of
Parliament, and inconsistent with the well government
of the State ": 101 Members voted *for,* and 216 *against*
the motion . . . If a member is said to be of Mr.
Hume's phalanx, it is meant that he is one of those
patriotic individuals who steadily supported Mr. Hume
in his various motions for the Reduction of the
Estimates and Establishments . . . Those who voted
for the repeal of the Salt Tax and the Window Tax,
for the reduction of the *Lay Lords* of the Admiralty,

of the Double Postmaster-General, *against* the Irish Tithe System, for the reduction of 10,000 men in the army, for inquiry into the third class of Civil-List expenditure . . . are noticed. The members who voted in 1821, for inquiry into the Manchester outrage, for Mr. Lambton's motion on Parliamentary Reform, and for the repeal of the *Six Acts*, are also mentioned. By the repeal of the *Six Acts* is meant the Act for the prevention of "*Seditious Meetings*" and "the Blasphemous and Seditious Libel Act"; these are the only *two*, out of the *Six Acts*, for the repeal of which any motion has been made.

27: JOHN FOSTER: Letter to John Easthope, M.P., May 23, 1827

CAN you be perfectly free from all suspicion . . . when you, the whole tribe of you, patriots, reformers, democrats, and what not, find yourselves suddenly transported . . . from your warlike position, in *front* of Canning, to a station of alliance and fighting co-operation beside him and behind him, while he has not made so much as a hypocritical profession of any change of principles or measures? The riddance of a good quantity of the most rotten aristocracy from the administration is plainly enough a good thing, so far. But we folks, who are at a great distance from the grand central monopoly of wisdom . . . cannot well comprehend this zealous coalition of the avowed enemies of all corruption with a minister who has been, through all times and seasons, its friend and defender, and more than so, fairly tells them . . . that he will continue in his old course, explicitly scouting beforehand their parliamentary reform, their attempts in behalf of the Dissenters, and all that. To *us* it would really seem . . . that the reformers, economizers, &c., are consenting to forego all their best projects, and even principles, for the honour of being denominated . . . " his honourable friends " . . .

" But Catholic Emancipation! Catholic Emancipation! " Why, yes,—very well so far, if that, even so much as *that*, were in any likelihood to be affected; but this worthy Minister has consented to abandon even that to its feeble and remote chance. For, as left to its own shifts, what chance has it in the Lords?

But even supposing this most virtuous and patriotic Minister, backed by his scores of converts and new friends, could, would, and did carry this measure what then? Will he alleviate the oppressive burdens of the country? Will he cut down the profligate and enormous expenditure of the government? Will he bring any of the detestable public delinquents to justice? Will he blow up a single rotten borough? Will he rout out that infernal Court of Chancery? Will he do anything toward creating an effective police throughout the country . . . ? Or (to glance abroad) will he do anything for Greece, or anything to real, effectual purpose, for . . . the Peninsula? Nay, will he do anything at last for even amendment of the West Indies, which he has palavered about so much? . . .

(*John Foster's Life and Correspondence*, 1846)

28: JOHN WADE: DEDICATION TO THE PEOPLE OF THE
Extraordinary Black Book or Reformer's Bible,
February 1, 1831

(In a new edition, John Wade warns the Grey
Government against " tinkering" with Reform)

To the People our labours may be fitly inscribed—
they are the tribunal of last resort—also the victims of
misrule,—and to them, therefore, may be properly
dedicated a record of the abuses from which they have
long suffered . . .

All the blessings the nation ought to enjoy have been
intercepted,—the rewards of industry, science, and
virtue have been dissipated in iniquitous wars abroad—
at home, in useless establishments, in Oligarchical
luxury, folly and profusion.

If we wanted proof of misgovernment—of incapacity and turpitude—Ireland affords a frightful
example: it is not Mr. O'Connell who causes her
agitation; he is only one of the fruits of Tyranny, an
effect, not the cause, of the disorders, which have
originated in the neglect of her vast resources, in an
unemployed population, an absentee proprietary, and
a plundering church. To the wretchedness of Ireland,
England is fast approaching . . . It is not the manufacturing, but the agricultural districts which are now
excited; these have always formed the exclusive domain
of the Clergy and Aristocracy; the rural population
is exactly what tithes, game-laws, the county
magistracy, Church-of-Englandism, and a luxurious
and non-resident priesthood have made them. And
what do we behold? The people have risen against
their pastors and landlords, and have resorted to nightly

outrage and revenge—the last resort of the oppressed for wrongs for which neither remedy nor inquiry has been vouchsafed.

We are not of the number of those who inculcate patient submission to undeserved oppression. A favourite toast of Dr. Johnson was, " Success to an insurrection of the Blacks." Shall we say—Success to the rising of the Whites! We should at once answer yes, did we not think some measure would be speedily adopted to mitigate the bitter privations and avert the further degradation of the labouring classes.

A new era, we are told, is about to commence: — no more liberticide wars—no more squanderings of the produce of industry in sinecures and pensions—and, above all, reform is to be conceded. We wait in patience. Our diseases are manifold, but the last is the initiative of all the rest, involving at once the destruction of partial interests—of monopolies, corn-laws, judicial abuse, unequal taxation,—and giving full weight and expression to the general weal and intelligence. If Ministers are honest, they deserve and will require all the support the People can give them to overturn a system which is the reverse: if they are not, they will be soon passed under the ban of their predecessors, with the additional infamy of having deceived . . . We have hope but no confidence.

Public opinion, and not Parliament, is *omnipotent*; it is that which has effected all the good which has been accomplished, and it is that which must effect the remainder. Unfortunately, Government can never be better constituted than it is for the profit of those who share in its administration; they have no interest in *change*, and their great maxims of rule are,—first, to concede nothing, so long as it can with *safety* be refused; secondly, to concede as little as possible; and, lastly, only to concede that little when every pretext for delay and postponement has been exhausted. Such are the arcana of those from whom reform is to proceed, and it is unnecessary to suggest the watchfulness, unanimity, and demonstrations by which they must be opposed.

Some of the Ministers are honest—they are all ingenious, and, no doubt, will have an ingenious plan, with many ingenious arguments for its support, concocted for our acceptance . . . and, perhaps, endeavour, to substitute the shadow for the substance! But it will avail them nothing; the balance is deranged, and it must be adjusted by a real increase of democratic power. The remedy, too, must be one of *immediate* action . . . it must not be patch-work—no disfranchising of non-resident voters—the transfer of the right of voting to great towns—the lessening of election expenses—and stuff of that sort. Such tinkering will not merit discussion . . .

We have fully stated our views on the subject in the concluding article of our work: our chief points are the Ballot; the entire abolition of all existing rights of suffrage; the substitution of an uniform elective qualification; the shortening of the duration of Parliaments; and the number of representatives returned by each town or district to be proportioned to the number of electors.

These conditions granted, a real reform would be obtained, and all good would follow in their train. Our last wishes are, that the PEOPLE, to whom we dedicate our labours, will be firm—united—and persevering, and, rely upon it, we are on the eve of as great a social regeneration as the destruction of feudality, the abase-

ment of Popery, or any other of the memorable epochs
which have signalized the progress of nations.

29: *The Examiner,* Sunday, May 13, 1832

GRAND MEETING OF THE BIRMINGHAM POLITICAL UNION
AND OTHER UNIONS OF THE MIDLAND COUNTIES,
MONDAY, MAY 7

THE largest meeting ever collected on one spot for a
political object, was held at Birmingham, under the
auspices of the Union, in order to assist the king and
his ministers to accomplish their great measure of
reform forthwith, and to carry it into a law unimpaired
in all its . . . provisions. The meeting was assembled
at the foot of Newhall-hill, a large piece of waste
ground lying to the north of the town of Birmingham,
and exceedingly well adapted from its vast size and
amphitheatrical form for the purpose. The hustings
were erected at the lowest point of the ground so that
the speakers could be seen, if not heard, at the farthest
point of the field. About 10 o'clock the Political Unions
of Wolverhampton, Coventry, Warwick, Stratford,
Dudley, Bilston, Kidderminster, Studley, Redditch,
Willenhall, Walsall, Wednesbury, Stourbridge,
Darlaston, &c., accompanied by great numbers of the
country people, began to enter Birmingham, in separate
companies, preceded by banners and bands of music.
The following has been given as an authentic statement of the numbers which came into Birmingham
from the surrounding districts: "Grand Northern
Division, headed by Mr. Fryer, the banker, including
Wolverhampton, Bilston, Wednesbury, Sedgeley,
Walsall, Willenhall, Darlaston, West Bromwich, and

Handsworth. This division may at the very lowest be estimated at 100,000 people. The procession extended over four miles—Grand Western Division, including Stourbridge, Dudley, Harbourn, Cradley, Lyewater, Oldbury, Rowley, and Halesowen. The procession extended two miles, and the number of the people was 25,000.—Grand Eastern Division, including Coventry, Warwick, Bedworth, Kenilworth, Leamington, Solihull, &c. consisted of 5,000 people.—Grand Southern Division, including Worcester, Bromsgrove, Redditch, Studley, Droitwich, and Alcester consisted of 20,000 people. The preceding estimate is exclusive of the 140,000 inhabitants of Birmingham and its immediate vicinity. Upwards of 200 bands of music were in attendance, and from 700 to 1,000 banners waved over the assembled throng." The commencement of the proceedings was announced at half-past twelve o'clock, by sound of bugle.

Mr. Attwood was placed in the chair, amidst loud cheers . . . He congratulated the assembly . . . It was only necessary to stamp upon the earth, and instantly from above the ground and beneath the ground a hundred thousand brave men determined to see their country righted present themselves at the call . . . Mr. Fryer of Wolverhampton next presented himself . . . Mr. J. Scholefield . . . Mr. G. F. Muntz . . Mr. G. Edmonds . . . Mr. B. Hadley . . . Rev. Mr. M'Donnell . . . The Rev. Dr. Wade . . . Mr. J. Parkes . . . declared his firm belief that if Lord Grey should be driven from office, or the bill be mutilated, the Political Unions throughout the country would be trebled and quadrupled in numbers. . . . God forbid that he should excite them to the dernier resort of a civil and physical contention for their liberties, or that he should seek to influence British noblemen by any unworthy terror of revolution. . . . He implored the House of Lords not to force the reformers to a civil contest . . .

30: JAMES MILL: *Essay on Government*, 1821

THE end of Government has been described in a great variety of expressions. By Locke it was said to be " the public good "; by others it has been described as being "the greatest happiness of the greatest number " . . . To understand what is included in the happiness of the greatest number, we must understand what is included in the happiness of the individuals of whom it is composed . . . we may allow, for example, in general terms, that the lot of every human being is determined by his pain and pleasure: and that his happiness corresponds with the degree in which his pleasures are great and his pains are small . . . We may assume it . . . that the concern of Government . . . is to increase to the utmost the pleasures, and to diminish to the utmost the pains which men derive from one another . . .

Of the laws of nature, on which the condition of man depends, that which is attended with the greatest number of consequences is the necessity for labour for obtaining the means of subsistence, as well as the means of the greatest part of our pleasures. This is, no doubt, the primary cause of government, for, if nature had produced spontaneously all the objects which we desire, and in sufficient abundance . . . there would have been no sources of dispute . . . nor would any man have possessed the means of ever acquiring authority over another.

The results are exceedingly different, when nature produces the objects of desire not in sufficient abundance for all. The source of dispute is then exhaustless . . . In this case, the end to be obtained, through Government as the means would be, to make that distribution of the scanty materials of happiness which would insure the greatest sum of it in the members of the community taken altogether.

An element of great importance is taken into the calculation when it is considered that most of the objects of desire, and even the means of subsistence, are the product of labour. The means of insuring labour must, in that case, be provided for as the foundation of all.

The means for the insuring of labour are of two sorts . . . the first sort is commonly denominated force: and under its application, the labourers are slaves. This mode of procuring labour we need not consider; for if the end of Government is to produce the greatest happiness of the greatest number, that end cannot be attained by making the greatest number slaves.

The other mode of obtaining labour is by allurement, or the advantage which it brings. If we would obtain all the objects of desire in the greatest possible quantity, we must obtain labour in the greatest possible quantity and, if we would obtain labour in the greatest possible quantity, we must raise the advantage attached to labour to the greatest possible height. It is impossible to attach to labour a greater degree of advantage than the whole product of labour. Why so? Because if you give more to one man than the produce of his labour, you can do so only by taking it away from the produce of some other man's labour. The greatest possible happiness of society is, therefore, obtained by insuring to every man the greatest possible quantity of the produce of his own labour . . .

How is this to be accomplished? For it is obvious that every man who has not all the objects of his desire, has inducement to take them from any other man who is weaker than himself . . . And how is this to be prevented? One mode is sufficiently obvious: and it does not appear that there is any other. It is the union of a certain number of men, agreeing to protect one another . . . and delegate to a small number the power necessary for protecting them all . . . This is Government. And it thus appears that it is for the sake of property that Government exists. . . .

All the difficult questions of Government relate to the means of restraining those in whose hands are lodged the powers necessary for the protection of all, from making a bad use of it. There are three modes in which it may be supposed that the powers of protecting the community are capable of being exercised . . . the Democratical, the Aristocratical, and the Monarchical . . . Of the forms of Government, which have been called the three simple forms, not one is adequate to the ends which Government is appointed to secure . . . the community itself, which alone is free from motives opposite to those ends, is incapacitated by its numbers from performing the business of Government; and—whether Government is entrusted to one or a few, they have not only motives opposite to those ends, but motives which will carry them, if unchecked, to the greatest evils . . .

In the grand discovery of modern times, the system of representation, the solution of all the difficulties . . . will perhaps be found . . . If there is both a King and an Aristocracy . . . the checking body must have sufficient power successfully to resist the united power of both King and Aristocracy . . . The grand difficulty consists in finding the means of constituting a checking body, whose powers shall not be turned against the community for whose protection it is created. There can be no doubt that if power is granted to a body of men called Representatives, they, like all other men, will use their power, not for the advantage of the community, but for their own advantage if they can. The only question is, therefore, how they can be prevented? in other words, how are the interests of the Representatives to be identified with those of the Community?

. . . limiting the duration of their power is a security against the sinister interest of the people's Representatives . . . The check of the short period for which he is chosen, and during which he can promote his sinister interest, is the same upon the man who has been chosen, and rechosen twenty times as upon the man who has been chosen for the first time. (Implied support here for annual or, at most, biennial elections) . . .

. . . if a small number of men have the choice of Representatives, such Representatives will be chosen as will promote the interests of that small number, by reducing, if possible, the rest of the community to be the abject and helpless slaves of their will . . . The Representative system is, in that case, only an operose and clumsy machinery for doing that which might as well be done without it; namely reducing the community to subjection under the one or the few. When we say the few,—it is of no importance whether we mean a few hundreds or a few thousands; or even *many* thousands . . . A numerous Aristocracy has never been found to be less oppressive than an Aristocracy confined to a few.

The general conclusion, therefore . . . is this; that

the benefits of the Representative system are lost, in all cases in which the interests of the choosing body are not the same with those of the community.

It is very evident, that if the community itself were the choosing body, the interest of the community and that of the choosing body would be the same. The question is whether that of any portion of the community, if erected into the choosing body, could remain the same! . . . All those individuals whose interests are indisputably included in those of other individuals may be struck off without inconvenience—all children to a certain age . . . women . . . the interest of all of whom is involved either in that of their fathers or in that of their husbands . . .

Having ascertained that an interest identical with that of the whole community is to be found in the aggregate males, of an age to be regarded as *sui juris*, persons who may be regarded as the virtual Representatives of the whole population, we have to go on and inquire whether this requisite quality may not be found in some lesser number . . .

(This was a reprint from the article on *Government* written for the *Encyclopaedia Britannica*.)

31 : JEREMY BENTHAM: *Parliamentary Candidate's Proposed Declaration of Principles,* 1831

CANDIDATE'S DECLARATION OF PRINCIPLES . . .

I. Ends aimed at . . .

I recognize, as the . . . only right and proper end of Government, the greatest happiness of the members of the community in question: the greatest happiness of all of them, without exception, in so far as possible: the greatest happiness of the greatest number of them, on every occasion on which the nature of the case renders the provision of an equal quantity of happiness for every one of them impossible . . .

These same incontrovertible ends of all good government, I once more acknowledge . . . and recapitulate: *Greatest happiness maximized; national subsistence, abundance, security and equality maximized; official aptitude maximized: expense, in all shapes, minimized.*

II. Appetites guarded against . . .

III. Economy and Uncorruption promised . . .

IV. Useful Knowledge to all promised . . .

V. Notoriety of Law to all promised . . .

VI. Justice, accessible to all, promised . . .

VII. Impartiality in Elections promised . . .

VIII. In International Dealings, Justice and Beneficence promised . . .

Never will I seek to add to the opulence or power of this our state, at the expense of the opulence or power of any other state, any otherwise than, in the competition between individual and individual, each may, without injury, seek to advance his own prosperity in preference to that of the other.

All profit by *conquest* in every shape, I acknowledge to be no other than robbery: robbery having murder for its instrument . . . robbery, committed by the ruling few in the conquering nation, on the subject many in both nations: robbery, of which, by the expense of armament, the people of the conquering nation are the first victims . . .

Seeing, that in all war, it is only through the sides of the unoffending many that the guilty few can ever receive a wound—never will I, for any other purpose than that of national self-defence, or receipt of compensation for pecuniary damage actually sustained, consent to make war on any other state: nor yet for pecuniary damage, till all endeavours for the obtainment of compensation . . . are hopeless: nor unless, if not prevented by war, future injury, to a greater amount . . . is actually apprehended by me.

Never will I consent to the receiving, or even retaining, under the dominion of this our state—even though it were at the desire of the inhabitants—any portion of territory, situate at any such distance . . . as to prevent any of the wants of the inhabitants . . . from receiving . . . relief as effectual as that which they could receive . . . regarding, as I do, all such dominion, as no better than an instrument, and device, for the accumulation of patronage and oppressive power, in the hands of the ruling few in the dominating state, at the expense, and by the sacrifice, of the interest and felicity of the subject many, in both states.

No recognition of superiority on the part of this our state, in relation to any other state, will I ever seek to procure, or consent to receive . . .

I acknowledge all such words as honour, glory, and dignity, when so employed, to be words of delusion, employed by rulers for the purpose of engaging subject citizens to consent, or submit, to be led, for the purpose of depredation, to the commission of murder upon the largest scale . . .

(This sixpenny pamphlet was reproduced from Chapter 7 of Bentham's *Constitutional Code; for the use of all Nations and all Governments professing Liberal Opinions.*)

PART IV

RADICALISM, ULTRA-RADICALISM AND CHARTISM

1832–1848

RADICALISM, ULTRA-RADICALISM
AND CHARTISM

1832–1848

As is well known, the Reform Bill, and the Reformed
Parliament assembled under it in January 1833, were
far from realising the hopes of the enthusiasts. Some
important changes were carried against steadily
stiffening Tory opposition in the years between
1833 and 1840, but nothing like the full newspaper
and hustings programmes so confidently put
forward in 1832. A typical newspaper programme of
the time, extracted from the *Brighton Guardian's*
Radical columns of December 1832, is printed as
Document 32, and then follows, in Document 33, a
Radical pessimist's far-sighted view of the true facts
of the situation. Unfortunately, the leaders of the
" Parliamentary Radicals " of 1833–41, not excepting
the vain and irritable Lord Durham (No. 34), fell far
below the requisite standards of intellectual weight and
political ability for what would, in any case, have been
the immense task of wresting the political leadership
of the country from Whigs and Tories alike. In the
next decade, Cobden was able to achieve such a miracle
in a limited economic field, but during the 1830s the
" Parliamentary Radicals " not only failed to produce a
Cobden or a Bright but anybody in Parliament of the
calibre of outside Radicals like Parkes and Place, fated,
as shown in No. 35, to act exclusively behind the

scenes. The Parliamentary Radicals' poverty in first-class personalities is made abundantly clear in John Stuart Mill's well-known account in his *Autobiography*, printed as No. 36. Even when the great slump of 1837–41 overtook the country and brought widespread unemployment and hunger in its train, it was not to the "Parliamentary Radicals" that the middle-class electorate turned for salvation from Whig ineffectiveness, but to Peel.

The working classes were hardly likely, in view of past history, to turn to the Tories with any enthusiasm. Their support had, in fact, for years been divided between the agitation for the "People's Charter" and that for the Repeal of the Corn Laws. Although both these agitations were Radical enough from the point of view of the Whig Front Bench of 1839, that against the Corn Laws (represented by the extracts from Cobden in No. 39), was sufficiently narrow in scope and led with sufficient ability and "respectability" to capture, by 1846, a probable majority of the restricted electorate.

Very different was the fate of the Chartist agitation. It became early associated in the public mind with incendiary oratory, mob processions and threats of "Physical Force". To have granted the Chartists' Six Points would have been to hand over Parliament, and with it the complete control of the national resources, to ignorant and illiterate mobs and to leaders almost certain to be pushed to confiscatory policies of the most sweeping kind, policies that would have far outdistanced those of the Jacobins. It seems most unlikely that Bronterre O'Brien[1] or any other of the Chartist leaders saw as far forward as this, and certainly the Chartist

[1] An illustration of O'Brien's leadership is given in No. 37.

National Petitions, adopted in 1839, 1842, and 1848 (Nos. 38, 41, and 43), are concerned with different and more immediate considerations. The 1839 Petition was by far the best-written of Chartist documents and seems to have come mainly from the pen of Douglas, editor of the *Birmingham Journal*. He was closely connected with the Radical groups of Midland industrialist politicians who had played a vital part in forcing through the Reform Bill and who now wished to start a new popular agitation, combining masters and men, as in the Political Unions, to end the bitter trade depression by freeing the " circulating medium " from rigid attachment to gold. It must be supposed that these Radical- industrialists, led by Thomas Attwood, the Birmingham M.P., considered that they could keep the new movement in leash as once they had kept the Birmingham Political Union. But they soon learned their mistake, Douglas among the first. Nevertheless, in 1842, a number of members of the Anti-Corn-Law League were again experimenting with a Complete Suffrage Movement (No. 40) designed to unite middle-class and working-class radicals and to heal the sharp divisions and distrust between the Anti-Corn-Law League with its largely middle-class following and the working-class Chartists.

The Complete Suffrage Movement failed and Chartism pursued an independent course until it dwindled away at the end of the 1840s. The Chartist National Petition of 1842 makes a poor comparison with that of 1839, yet it mirrors perhaps a good deal more truly than the earlier Petition the grievances which the working man in the pit, factory or brickyard was readiest to seize on. Feargus O'Connor's *Northern Star* was directed to the same audience, a call to the

"Fustian Jackets, the Blistered Hands, and Unshorn Chins". Such demagogic tactics, however, whilst they sold the paper and packed O'Connor's meetings, were a grave weakness in Chartist leadership. This seems to have been felt when the Chartists drew up their 1848 Petition (No. 43), for in place of the wide range of complaint characteristic of the 1842 Petition, this concentrated on the case for the Six Points—universal suffrage, vote by ballot, equal electoral districts, payment of members, annual parliaments, and the abolition of any property qualification for members. The case was scarcely put with skill or eloquence, though it was not this weakness which killed the petition, but the gross exaggeration which claimed over 5,700,000 signatures when there were in reality under 2,000,000—and many of these fictitious.

A document in this section (No. 42) illustrates another of the most interesting sides of Chartism, O'Connor's attempt to organise a land settlement scheme. The experiment was actually launched, but failed after a short time.

32: *The Brighton Guardian,* 1832

WE would destroy, the instant it was possible, the House and Window Tax, because they are unequal, and the people hate them. We would destroy the Malt Tax and the Hop Duty, because they impede the cultivation of the land and subject tradesmen and farmers to a rigorous and despotic system of excise. We would destroy the Tax on Soap, because it is a bounty on dirt and disease; as we would destroy the Taxes on Knowledge, because they are bounties on ignorance and error. We would destroy the monopolies of the Bank of England, and of the East India Company, because they tax the whole community for the exclusive benefit of the proprietors of Bank and East India stock, and subject all commerce to be deranged by the caprice of individuals, against which open and public and general competition is the only sure and certain guarantee. We would destroy the Corn Laws, because they cheat the farmer with a hope of prices he never realises, and make him promise a higher rent than he can pay,— because they tend to starve the poor . . . manufacturers—and because they do not even benefit those landlords whom they merely flatter with preserving for them a nominal superiority which must come to an end. We would destroy the power of parsons and other justices to interfere with all the pastimes and amusements of the people . . . We would destroy every pension not earned by useful public services. We would destroy every public office which is not indispensable for the real service of the public; limiting the whole action of the Government to the one great duty of protecting the property of individuals.

(Quoted in *The Examiner*, December 16, 1832.)

33: JOHN FOSTER: Letter to John Easthope, M.P., February 8, 1833

FOR myself, when I look at the dreadful array of affairs which our legislators have before them, and pressing on them close, and thick, and immediate, I am the reverse of sanguine, whether I regard the question of *power* or of *will*. There is that most appalling state of Ireland. I have no degree of confidence that the ministry have even the *will* to adopt the bold, and radical, and comprehensive measures which alone could avail there. How obvious is the necessity for some imperious enactment, to compel that base, detestable landed interest to take the burden of the poor, instead of driving them out to famish, beg, or rob, and murder, on the highway; or throwing them by tens of thousands on our coast, to devour the means of support to our own population. It would be a measure which would first astound, but speedily enrage the whole selfishly base proprietary of Ireland. I have no hope that the ministry have the resolution for so mighty a stroke: and then the Irish *church*. The plain sense of the thing is, that about two-thirds, or rather four-fifths of it, ought to be cut down at once, and that proportion of the property applied to national uses. But the very notion of such a thing would be enough to consign —— to one of the wards in St. Luke's. And what would —— say, if Lord Grey dared even to whisper such a thing to him? And yet, unless some such thing be done, it is as clear as noon-day, that Ireland will continue a horrid scene of distraction and misery; growing, month by month, more ferociously barbarous, and to be kept down by nothing but the terror and occasional exploits of an immense standing army . . .

(*John Foster's Life and Correspondence*, 1846)

34: Lord Durham: Two Speeches, 1834

At Edinburgh, September 13, 1834

I AM AWARE that there are men who feel considerable apprehension from the increasing privileges given to classes who have not hitherto enjoyed them. I feel no such distrust . . . I look at their industry and intelligence, and I repose with perfect confidence in their conduct [Cheering]: but, be that as it may, I contend that it was necessary that the experiment should be made. In early times, government went on without the people; in the next period, it went on in despite of the people; and now the experiment has been tried whether it cannot go on with the people [Cheers]. . . One word more and I have done. My noble and learned friend, the Lord Chancellor, has been pleased to give some sound advice to certain classes of persons . . . whom he considers as evincing too much impatience. I will freely own to you that I am one of those who see with regret every hour which passes over the existence of acknowledged and unreformed abuses. [Rapturous applause] . . . I object to the clipping, and the paring and the mutilating, which must inevitably follow any attempt to conciliate enemies, who are not to be gained [Great cheering], and who will requite your advances by pointing out your inconsistency, your abandonment of your friends and principles, and then ascribe the discontent created in our own ranks by those proceedings, to the decay of liberal feelings in the country. Against such a course of proceedings I must ever protest [Cheering].

At Glasgow, October 29, 1834

For more than twenty years I have laboured honestly, zealously, and conscientiously in the public cause [Cheers]. I have never deviated . . . Every inducement has been tendered to me since I received your invitation, to prevent me from coming to meet you here this day [Immense cheering]. I was told, forsooth, that I should find your principles too violent, and that I should commit myself by listening to opinions which tend to the destruction of all good government [Cheers]. My answer to all this was unvarying. I denied that I should find any such principles here among the men of Glasgow [Cheers] ... I will avail myself of this opportunity to justify myself, which I will do [Great cheering] against these accusations. All I stated ... at Gateshead was, that Earl Grey had entrusted to me the preparation of the Reform Bill, and that I had been assisted in that task by three of my colleagues. Was that a secret? . . . it was notorious . . .

We have to require the perfecting of the Reform Act. We have to require the repeal of the Septennial Act [Cheers]. We have to require the purification of the Church Establishments of England and Ireland from all acknowledged abuses [Long continued cheering]. We have to demand the reform of corporation abuses in England, and the strictest continuance in economy and retrenchment [Cheers]. No doubt there are many other measures emanating from these to which I have alluded, and on which my sentiments are well known . . . I assert that the true result of timely and not too long delayed reform, is to preserve all that is valuable by removing all that is corrupt in our institutions [Immense cheering] . . .

These are my opinions, and these are my principles . . . I would not accept the highest office in the gift of the Crown; I would not even receive the warm enthusiastic approbation of you, my fellow-countrymen, if either were gained . . . by the compromise of a single principle [Cheers] . . .

(*Speeches of the Rt. Hon. the Earl of Durham, 1836*)

35 : JOSEPH PARKES: Letter to Francis Place, 1836

A letter from Joseph Parkes, one of the leading Birmingham Radicals, to Francis Place, perhaps the best known of the Radical leaders in London between 1806 and the 1830s. The letter was written early in 1836, when the Municipal Reform Act, on which the two Radicals had long co-operated, was yielding its first results. From the Place MSS. in the British Museum, quoted by Jessie K. Buckley in *Joseph Parkes of Birmingham*.

THIS night closes about two and a half years of as much mental and physical work and of as much anxiety and responsibility . . . as most *young* men ever went through in *this* country. But the postscript to the Reform Bills of 1832 is carried and in wholesome action. This week . . . has fired the people in England and Wales with a real love of democracy and self-government. Far from perfect as the Corporation Act was and reduced as was its original degree of perfection—yet it has done, or rather will in its effects *do the business* and that at no distant time. The unincorporated towns will lust after and soon accomplish the destruction of their Self-Elect and the county Magisterial and Fiscal Self-Elect will next and early be mowed down by the Scythe of Reform. The *Franchise* you and I knew would do the trick and must lead to a Uniformity and extension of Parliamentary franchise. The new Town Councils are of course compounded of much local Whiggism, a deleterious ingredient. But the Rads will in a year or two work all that scum off. Three years are only a moment in the life of a nation.

You write me about parties . . . All the gangs are what they have ever been. Tories are burked, no resurrection for them. Whigs will, of course, raise their bidding with the People's growing power and demand. They are an unnatural party standing between the

People and the Tory aristocracy chiefly for the pecuniary value of offices and vanity of power. Their hearse is ordered. Wait dear old friend from whom I early (a raw uneducated boy) learned much *honest and sound*. Be in no hurry. *You* have put many a nail into the coffin of party. Be in no hurry. We must keep up a Jury mast to get into Port and goad on but not destroy the rickety, brainless, opinionless Ministry. It has been made the instrument of Corporation Abuses. Let us get one for Ireland . . . and something next session for England and Wales which I must not mention. . . .

36: J. S. Mill: *Autobiography*

In the meanwhile had taken place the election of the first Reformed Parliament, which included several of the most notable of my Radical friends and acquaintances—Grote, Roebuck, Buller, Sir William Molesworth, John and Edward Romilly, and several more; besides Warburton, Strutt, and others who were in Parliament already. Those who thought themselves, and were called by their friends, the philosophic Radicals, had now, it seemed, a fair opportunity . . . and I, as well as my father, founded great hopes on them. These hopes were destined to be disappointed . . . they left the lead of the Radical portion of the House to the old hands, to Hume and O'Connell . . . And now, on a calm retrospect, I can perceive that the men were less in fault than we supposed, and that we had expected too much from them. They were in unfavourable circumstances. Their lot was cast in the ten years of inevitable reaction, when, the Reform excitement being over, and the few legislative improvements which the public really called for having been rapidly effected, power gravitated back in its natural direction, to those who were for keeping things as they were ... It would have required a great political leader, which no one is to be blamed for not being, to have really effected great things by parliamentary discussion when the nation was in this mood. My father and I had hoped that some competent leader might arise; some man of philosophic attainments and popular talents, who could have put heart into the many younger or less distinguished men that would have been ready to join him—could have made them available, to the extent of their talents, in bringing advanced ideas before the public—could have used the House of Commons ... for instructing and impelling the public mind; and would either have forced the Whigs to receive their measures from him, or have taken the lead of the Reform party out of their hands. Such a leader there would have been, if my father had been in Parliament. For want of such a man the instructed Radicals sank into a mere *Côté Gauche* of the Whig party....

What I could do by writing I did.... In the conduct of the (London) *Review* I had two objects. One was to free philosophic Radicalism from the reproach of sectarian Benthamism. I desired, while retaining the precision of expression, the definiteness of meaning, the contempt of declamatory phrases ... which were so honourably characteristic both of Bentham and of my father, to give a wider basis and a more free and genial character to Radical speculation ... In this first object I, to a certain extent, succeeded. The other thing I attempted was to stir up the educated Radicals, in and out of Parliament, to exertion, and induce them to make themselves—what I thought by using the proper means they might become—a powerful party capable of taking the government of the country, or at least of dictating the terms on which they would share it with the Whigs. The attempt was from the first chimerical . . . as Austin so truly said, " the country did not contain the men ".

(John Stuart Mill's *Autobiography* (1873), Chapter 6, 1830–1840 (Longman))

37: R. G. GAMMAGE: *History of Chartism*

MR. HETHERINGTON perceived the advantage that would accrue to the cause by securing Mr. O'Brien as a writer, and he accordingly became the editor of the *Poor Man's Guardian* . . . and it was through this journal that the worth of O'Brien, as a public writer, became known and appreciated. He also contributed powerful articles to *The Twopenny Dispatch, The People's Conservative, The Destructive* and other papers. The immense excitement which these papers caused will be well remembered by the politicians of that period. The Government tried every available means to put them down; not so much from a consideration of revenue, as from a fear of the progress of the doctrines they contained. In 1836, O'Brien made further progress in democratic literature, by the publication of a translated work entitled, *Buonarotti's History of Babeuf's Conspiracy for Equality.* O'Brien held that all the previous so-called histories of the French Revolution . . . blackened and traduced the character of the people's best, most humane, and enlightened friends . . . Shortly after the publication of this work, Mr. O'Brien paid a visit to Paris, partly for the purpose

of collecting information which should enable him to
write a true and faithful life of Robespierre, whose
character he conceived had been most foully and
shamelessly belied . . . Although other men had taken
upon themselves the initiation of the movement for the
Charter, it was the writings of O'Brien that laid the
foundation for that movement, and his great share in
the work was acknowledged as soon as the agitation had
fairly set in. As soon as the holding of a Convention
became settled, he was invited by no less than thirteen
constituencies to represent them . . .

As an orator O'Brien . . . spoke not in the flowing
style of Vincent, nor in the rapid declamatory strain
of O'Connor, nor were his addresses always marked by
the measured deliberateness of Lowery; but he
combined in a measure the advantages of all three.
O'Brien's speech [at the West Riding Meeting on Peep
Green "when 200,000 assembled"] was full of
valuable matter . . . Towards the conclusion . . . he
said:

"At the next general election we must have Chartists
as our representatives, and when they have been elected
by a show of hands, we must insist on having a formal
return to that effect made by the returning officer. We
shall thus have a parliament legally chosen by the
Queen's writ, and we shall then show our tyrants the
difference between a parliament nominated by nine or
ten millions, and one elected by three or four hundred
thousand monopolists. The people's parliament will
meet at Birmingham, and then it may be necessary that
50,000 of their constituents shall proceed thither, to
protect them in the discharge of their legislative duties,
and then when they are all thus assembled, then I will
tell you what I mean to do, but not till then . . . You

support the whole tribe of landholders, fundholders, and 2,000,000 of menials and kept mistresses, together with 100,000 prostitutes in London alone. Why should you not have institutions to make these people get their living honestly? Universal suffrage would at once put the remedy within your grasp . . . The national petition will be a notice to quit, and they will very shortly be served with a process of ejectment. I will now conclude by earnestly entreating you to co-operate with the General Convention, and above all things to avoid premature and partial outbreaks. For myself, wherever I may be, and whatever may become of me,—and I understand there is a warrant out against me,—I shall to my latest breath advocate the principle, that the people ought only to be governed by the people themselves."

(Op. cit., 1854, p. 81 et sqq.)

38: THE CHARTISTS' PETITION, 1839

To the Honourable the Commons of Great Britain and Ireland, in Parliament assembled, the Petition of the undersigned, their suffering countrymen,

HUMBLY SHEWETH.—

That we, your petitioners, dwell in a land whose merchants are noted for their enterprise, whose manufacturers are very skilful, and whose workmen are proverbial for their industry. The land itself is goodly, the soil rich, and the temperature wholesome. It is abundantly furnished with the materials of commerce and trade. It has numerous and convenient harbours. In facility of internal communication it exceeds all others. For three and twenty years we have enjoyed a profound peace. Yet, with all the elements of national prosperity . . . we find ourselves overwhelmed with public and private suffering. We are bowed down under a load of taxes, which, notwithstanding, fall greatly short of the wants of our rulers. Our traders are trembling on the verge of bankruptcy; our workmen are starving. . . . The home of the artificer is desolate, and the warehouse of the pawnbroker is full. The workhouse is crowded, and the manufactory is deserted. We have looked on every side; we have searched diligently in order to find out the causes of distress so sore and so long continued. We can discover none in nature or in Providence. Heaven has dealt graciously by the people . . . but the foolishness of our rulers has made the goodness of God of none effect. The energies of a mighty kingdom have been wasted in building up the power of selfish and ignorant men . . . The few have governed for the interest of the few, while the interests of the many have been sottishly neglected, or insolently and tyrannously trampled upon. It was the fond expectation of the friends of the people, that a remedy for the greater part, if not for the whole of their grievances, would be found in the Reform Act of 1832. . . . They have been bitterly and basely deceived. The fruit which looked so fair to the eye, has turned to dust and ashes when gathered. The Reform Act has effected a transfer of power from one domineering faction to another, and left the people as helpless as before. . . .

We come before your honourable house to tell you, with all humility, that this state of things must not be permitted to continue. That it cannot long continue, without very seriously endangering the stability of the

throne, and the peace of the kingdom . . . We tell
your honourable house, that the capital of the master
must no longer be deprived of its due profit; that the
labour of the workman must no longer be deprived of
its due reward. That the laws which make food dear,
and the laws which make money scarce, must be
abolished. That taxation must be made to fall on
property, not on industry. That the good of the many,
as it is the only legitimate end, so must it be the sole
study of the government. As a preliminary essential
to these and other requisite changes—as the means by
which alone the interests of the people can be
effectually vindicated and secured, we demand that
those interests be confided to the keeping of the
people . . . If the self-government of the people should
not remove their distresses, it will, at least, remove their
repinings. Universal suffrage will, and it alone can,
bring true and lasting peace to the nation; we firmly
believe that it will also bring prosperity.

May it therefore please your honourable house, to
take this our petition into your most serious consideration, and to use your utmost endeavours . . . to have a
law passed, granting to every male of lawful age, sane
mind, and unconvicted of crime, the right of voting for
members of parliament and directing all future
elections . . . to be in the way of secret ballot, and
ordaining that the duration of parliament so chosen,
shall in no case exceed one year, and abolishing all
property qualifications in the members, and providing
for their due remuneration . . .

(R. G. Gammage, op. cit., pp. 96–98)

39: RICHARD COBDEN: Speech in the House of Commons, February 24, 1842

THE great body of those who legislated in 1815 . . . every party in the house, and many out of doors, were deceived; but there was one party which was not deluded—the party most interested in the question—namely the working classes. They were not deluded . . . Therefore it was, that when that law was passed your house was surrounded by the excited populace of London, and you were compelled to keep back an enraged people from your doors by the point of the bayonet [Cheers] . . . The disturbances were not confined to London; but throughout the north of England, from 1815 to 1819, when the great meeting took place on Peter's field, there never was a meeting in the North of England in which banners were not displayed with inscriptions of " No corn laws ". There was no mistake in the minds of the multitudes upon this question . . . There never was, and there is not now. They may not indeed cry out exclusively for the repeal of the corn laws; they have looked beyond the question, and they have seen, at the same time, other evils greater even than this which they are now calling upon you to remedy; and when they raise the cry of universal suffrage and the people's charter, do not let hon. gentlemen opposite suppose, because the Anti-Corn-Law League may, perchance, have run into collision with the masses upon some points, that the people are consequently favourable to the existence of the corn laws . . .

Having patiently waited for twenty-five years, I think we are entitled at last to a clear explanation of the pretext upon which you tax the food of the people, for the acknowledged benefit of the landowners. The right honourable baronet tells us we must not be dependent upon foreigners for our supply, or that that dependence must be supplementary, that certain years produce enough of corn for the demand, and that we must legislate for the introduction of corn only when it is wanted . . . The right honourable baronet (Sir R. Peel) I apprehend knows more of the state of the country than most of his followers . . . He is not legislating in the dark, and this I will venture to tell him, that bad as he finds trade now, he will live (if he follows out the course in which he proposes to embark) to find it much worse . . . I own, indeed, that I heard in the right honourable baronet's second speech something like an apologetic tone . . . not being able to do all that he would do. That tone would be very well if the right honourable baronet had been forced into his present position by the people . . . then, with some shadow of fairness, he might resort to the plea that his position was a difficult one, and that he would do more if his party would permit him . . . I beg to call to the right hon. baronet's mind, that if he is now placed in a situation of difficulty, that difficulty was sought by himself . . . He told us at Tamworth, that, for years and years, aye, even from the passing of the Reform Bill, he had been engaged in reconstructing his party. I presume he knew of what materials that party was composed. I presume he was not ignorant of the fact that it consisted of monopolists of every kind; monopolists of religion, monopolists of the franchise, monopolists of sugar, monopolists of corn, monopolists of timber, monopolists of coffee [Hear, hear]. These were the parties that gathered around him, and out of which he was to construct his new parliament. They were fully alive to the occasion. They set to work to revive the old system of corruption. They bribed and they bought [Cheers and counter cheers]. Yes, they bribed, they bought, and they intimidated [Renewed cheering from both sides] until they found themselves in office, and the right hon. baronet at their head . . . Did he expect that this party had expended their funds and their labour . . . in order that they might . . . assist him to take away their monopolies? . . . I will now say a word to the gentlemen on this side of the house . . . There are gentlemen here who think that the corn laws ought to be repealed, but they cannot reconcile themselves to the immediate repeal . . . "We admit," say they, "the injustice which these laws inflict upon upwards of 25,000,000 of the people for the advantage of a select few; but inasmuch as some thousands of persons have a beneficial interest in this wrong inflicted upon the millions, we cannot suddenly deprive them of the advantage they possess." Now, with all due deference . . . I must be permitted to say that I think they are showing a very great sympathy for the few who are gaining, and vastly little sympathy indeed for the many who are suffering from the operation of these laws [Cheers] . . .

(From the Anti-Corn-Law League's penny pamphlet, *The Corn Laws: Speech of R. Cobden, Esq., M.P., in the House of Commons, on Thursday evening, February* 24, 1842. Eighteenth thousand. Revised)

40: *The Nonconformist,* April 13, 1842

THIS Conference hereby record their emphatic protest against class legislation, both in its principle and in its workings. While the parliamentary franchise is restricted by arbitrary limits, whilst a certain section of the community, be it more or less extensive, is entrusted with the exclusive possession of legislative power . . . there exists, in the opinion of this conference, no guarantee for fair and equitable government.

The principle which invests a class with the peculiar attribute of choosing the people's representatives has no foundation either in Christianity or in reason, and in operation has been found to be productive of the most baneful results . . . Experience has proved that the possessors of the franchise never have recognized the privilege they enjoy as held in trust for the advantage of the whole nation . . .

In the deliberate judgement of this conference the exclusion of any class from equal constitutional rights places that class in a position of political slavery . . .

In the view of this conference the interests of the nation at large have suffered incalculably from class legislation. Its evils may be seen in every department. It upholds, at an enormous expense, and to the serious injury of religion, a vast system of ecclesiastical despotism—it paralyzes our commerce by the most absurd and unjust restrictions—it has narrowed the markets to our toil-worn industry, while it has enhanced the price of those articles upon which industry must necessarily subsist. It has undertaken without scruple, and in violation of all laws human and divine, wars, draining the country both of blood and money, and has so adjusted the taxation which such wars have rendered necessary as to touch but lightly the princely fortunes of the rich, and to take from the poor well nigh half their hard-earned wages . . .

Therefore, under a deep impression of the many and grievous evils inflicted upon the community by class-legislation, and recognizing the solemn obligations which rest upon them as men guided by the principles of Christianity . . . this conference feel bound to exert themselves to put an end to the present exclusive system . . .

> (From *The Noncomformist,* April 13, 1842. This is the text of the resolution adopted by the Complete Suffrage Conference at Birmingham.)

41 : The Chartists' National Petition, 1842

To the Hon. the Commons of Great Britain and Ireland, in Parliament assembled,

The petition of the undersigned people of the United Kingdom showeth . . . that your hon. house, as at present constituted, has not been elected by, and acts irresponsibly of the people; and hitherto has only represented parties, and benefited the few, regardless of the miseries, grievances, and petitions of the many . . . that your petitioners instance in proof of their assertion that your hon. house has not been elected by the people, that the population of Great Britain and Ireland is at the present time about 26,000,000 of persons, and that yet, out of this number, little more than 900,000 have been permitted to vote in the recent elections . . .; that the existing state of representation is not only extremely limited and unjust, but unequally divided, and gives preponderating influence to landed and monied interests . . . that Guildford, with a population of 9,920 returns to Parliament as many members as the Tower Hamlets with a population of 300,000; Evesham, with a population of 3,998, elects as many representatives as Manchester, with a population of 200,000, and Buckingham, Evesham, Totness, Guildford, Honiton, and Bridport, with a total population of 23,000 return as many representatives as Manchester, Finsbury, the Tower Hamlets, Liverpool, Marylebone, and Lambeth, with a population of 1,400,000; these being but a very few instances of the enormous inequalities existing in what is called the representation of the country; that bribery, intimidation, corruption, perjury and riot prevail at all Parliamentary elections . . . that your petitioners complain that they are enormously taxed to pay the interest of what is called the national debt—a debt amounting at present to 800,000,000 of pounds—being only a portion of the enormous amount expended in cruel and expensive wars for the suppression of all liberty . . . that in England, Ireland, Scotland and Wales, thousands of people are dying from actual want; that your petitioners . . . perceive, with feelings of indignation, the determination of your hon. house to continue the Poor Law Bill in operation, notwithstanding the cruel and murderous effects . . . that your petitioners would direct the attention of your hon. house to the great disparity existing between the wages of the producing millions and the salaries of those whose comparative usefulness ought to be questioned . . . your petitioners have learned that Her Majesty receives daily for her private use the sum of £164 17s. 10d. . . . his Royal Highness Prince Albert . . . the sum of £104 2s. 0d. . . . the King of Hanover daily receives £57 10s. 0d. . . . the Archbishop of Canterbury . . . £52 10s. 0d. per day whilst thousands of the poor have to maintain their families upon an income not exceeding 2d. per head per day; that, notwithstanding the wretched and unparalleled conditions of the people, your hon. house has manifested no disposition to curtail the expenses of the state . . . that an unconstitutional police force is distributed all over the country, at enormous cost, to prevent the due exercise of the people's rights . . . that a vast and unconstitutional army is upheld at the public expense . . . likewise to intimidate the millions; that your petitioners complain that the hours of labour, particularly of the factory workers are protracted beyond the limits of human endurance, and that the wages earned . . . are inadequate to sustain the bodily strength . . . that your petitioners complain that upwards of £9,000,000 per annum are annually abstracted from them to maintain a church establishment from which they principally dissent . . . that your petitioners complain of many grievances borne by the people of Ireland and contend that they are fully entitled to a repeal of the legislative union . . . should your hon. house be pleased to grant your petitioners a hearing by representatives . . . your petitioners will be enabled to unfold a tale of wrong and suffering . . . which will create utter astonishment . . . that the people of Great Britain and Ireland have so long quietly endured their wretched condition, brought upon them, as it has been, by unjust exclusion from political authority . . . that your petitioners therefore, exercising their just constitutional right, demand that your hon. house, to remedy the many gross and rampant evils of which your petitioners complain, do immediately, without alteration, deduction or addition, pass into a law the document entitled "The People's Charter" which embraces the representation of male adults, vote by ballot, annual parliaments, no property qualification, payment of members and equal electoral districts . . .

(*The Times* of May 3, 1842)

42: FEARGUS O'CONNOR

March 1, 1845

To the Working Classes:

My Dear Friends,—Circumstances combine just now to induce me to return to the consideration of a subject from which I was driven by ignorance, assumption and over-zeal . . . When almost every scribbler who can hold a pen . . . makes abuse of me his daily work, I think I may be permitted to speak of myself. I have revived, advocated and pushed the democratic principle with perseverance and success. I have succeeded in creating a party capable of withstanding all the dangers of a long and continuous calm—the greatest dangers that can threaten a politician. There is little trouble in navigating a vessel going before the breeze in the open sea; but there is great anxiety about her management when becalmed amid shoals and rocks. We have been three years in the latter position . . . while the calm created by temporary " prosperity " has left us scarcely a breath to fill our canvas. Nothing that had not taken deep root in the minds of the majority of the people could have withstood the adverse circumstances to which the democratic principle has been subjected. The object sought to be attained from the accomplishment of democratic principles is " a fair day's wage for a fair day's work ", an object which never, never can be achieved, except through the application of the artificial " surplus " of labour to the cultivation of the soil. I defy any man on earth to point out to me any possible means of correcting the evils of " surplus " labour, even with the Charter, otherwise than by its application to the land . . .

So fully convinced am I of this fact that I am resolved on trying the experiment myself, but not for my own advantage: and I shall shortly promulgate a plan by which, in less than twelve weeks, I propose to locate a hundred men and their families in the first home colony. I do not mean in community: but as individual possessors and willing co-operators because they will see an interest in co-operation. The *political* test I mean to apply to membership, is that each shall be a paying member to the National Charter Association ... I believe that the Chartist mind of this country has now arrived at the reasoning point, and that it must have something practical to live on ...

... I may further be permitted to direct attention to popular apathy as the greatest of all our enemies ... I ask you to look at the weekly subscriptions for the support of men, who every one of them, as itinerating lecturers, would receive double the amount of wage that you have promised, but not paid them ... I tell you that it is positively dishonest and must be remedied.

I am, your faithful friend and servant,

FEARGUS O'CONNOR

(Letter to the working classes in the *Northern Star,* March 1, 1845)

43: THE CHARTISTS' NATIONAL PETITION, 1848

To the Hon. the Commons of Great Britain and Ireland in Parliament assembled.

We the undersigned inhabitants of the British Isles and subjects of the British Crown, thus avail ourselves of the constitutional privilege of submitting the consideration of our political rights and wrongs to your hon. house . . . the guardians of the civil, social, and religious rights of the people . . .

That your petitioners regard the Reform Bill as unjust, as it restricts the right of citizenship to one-seventh of the male adult community, and stamps the other six-sevenths with the stigma of political inferiority.

That the system which your petitioners arraign before the judgement of your hon. house renders seven men subservient to the will, caprice, and dominance of one; that it not only establishes the ascendancy of a small minority of the empire, but it invests a minority of the small enfranchised fraction with the power of returning a majority of your hon. house . . .

That your petitioners believing the principle of universal suffrage to be based on those eternal rights of man, which, although kept in abeyance, can neither be alienated or destroyed, appeal to your hon. house to make such organic reforms in our representative system as will make that principle the foundation upon which shall stand the Commons' House of Parliament . . .

That your petitioners, in order that the elector may possess perfect security in the exercise of his franchise, pray that the voting at elections for members of parliament be taken by ballot. Your petitioners, aware of the great coercion and corrupted power possessed by wealth and station over the poor elector, see no hope of securing purity of election and genuineness of representation but in throwing the protective mantle of the ballot over the electoral body.

That your petitioners regard the present inequality of representation to be opposed to common sense . . . They therefore appeal to your hon. house to remedy this defect in the legislative machinery, by the division of the country into equal electoral districts, assigning to each district one representative.

That your petitioners hold the Legislature, equally with the Executive, to be the servants of the people, and consequently entitled to remuneration at the public expense.

That your petitioners consider septennial Parliaments unjust as they prevent, for six years out of seven, those who are annually arriving at maturity, from exercising their right of suffrage. Your petitioners also consider that seven years is too long a term . . . a period that affords an opportunity to venal and time-serving men to promote their selfish interests at the expense of those whose welfare should be the ultimate aim of all their labours. Your petitioners, therefore, entreat your hon. house to create between the representative and the represented that salutary responsibility indispensable to good government, by the restoration of the ancient wholesome practice of annual parliaments.

That your petitioners complain that a seat in the Commons House of Parliament should be contingent upon the possession of property of any description . . . and, therefore, pray for the abolition of what is termed the " property " qualification.

That your petitioners respectfully direct your attention to the document entitled "The People's Charter " which embodies the principles and the details for securing the full and equitable representation of the male adult population, which document they earnestly pray your hon. house to forthwith enact as the law of the realm . . .

(*The Times,* April 6, 1848)

Part V

THE END OF CHARTISM: BRIGHT TAKES THE RADICAL LEAD

1848–1867

THE END OF CHARTISM:
BRIGHT TAKES THE RADICAL LEAD

1848–1867

No ACCOUNT of nineteenth-century Radicalism is complete without noting the sympathy that was lavished on every Continental revolution and the immediate hopes that were excited that "liberty" was about to take a final and permanent shape. No. 44 is a good example of the eager if superficial treatment given to the early news of the 1848 Revolutions. The stimulating effect such treatment had on Chartism and "Young Ireland" was profound. Great official exertions were, in fact, necessary, in April 1848, to prevent Chartists from attempting to imitate Continental seizures of power. The "middle-class Radicals" did their part when they brought forward an appeasing programme of Household Suffrage, Triennial Parliaments and Ballot, sometimes known as the "Little Charter", and erected a National Parliamentary and Financial Reform Association to agitate for it (No. 45). In No. 46 are made clear the shifts which the "Little Charter" was imposing, by 1851, on the failing O'Connor, now rapidly sinking into insanity but still trying to keep his hold on a distinct party.

No. 47 shows Radical opinion on foreign affairs taking a new turn after Russian power had helped on the forcible restoration of the old order in Germany,

Italy, Austria and Hungary, but had been successfully defied when England and America had united to encourage Turkey to release Kossuth. Here, too, are to be found new Radical hopes taking shape for a great anti-Russian crusade to sweep despotism off the entire Continent. It was these hopes which had a large part in forcing on the Crimean War, and when that war was opened hesitantly and conducted badly, a tempest of popular fury against " aristocratic misgovernment " in Britain was unleashed which, at one stage, threatened to sweep away Lord Palmerston's Cabinet as it had already swept Lord Aberdeen's. No. 49 is a typical example of the Radical attacks on the Cabinets of the time, while No. 50 gives a Radical programme of 1858, calculated, it was claimed, to prevent further " aristocratic " mismanagement in the future.

Nearly every working-class political group of the 1850s, and even of the 1860s, was dominated still by personalities who had won distinction or suffered arrest and imprisonment for their part in the stormier days of Chartist agitation. No. 48 quotes a defiant message of 1854 from one of these Chartist personalities: perhaps its most significant feature is the unashamed and unabashed " physical force " view still advocated. For four years more the attempt to keep a Chartist party together behind Ernest Jones and the *People's Paper* continued, but long before the *People's Paper* ended in September 1858, even the Chartist faithful seem to have been tiring of the complete inability of their movement to affect the Parliamentary scene. In this situation, Bright's famous oratorical campaign of 1858–9, organised though it was by a " middle-class Radical " Committee, was specially fitted to capture the attention and even the enthusiasm of working-class multitudes. Document 51 gives typical extracts from Bright's speeches. They reveal very well why his assaults on the vast mass of surviving political, fiscal and ecclesiastical privilege, enjoyed primarily by the landed aristocracy, were received with almost equal relish by moneyed industrialists (especially if they were Dissenters) and working-class Radicals, even the most "ultra". Soon Bright was being hailed in some Radical quarters (No. 52) not merely as a claimant to the Radical leadership but even as a possible Prime-Minister-to-be.

Bright's campaign had some effect in stimulating the offer of a tricky but abortive Reform Bill from Disraeli in 1859, and of an unsatisfactory Whig Bill in 1860, but it was in 1866 that the opportunity at last opened for a new Bright agitation that should be successful as well as resounding.

Bright had reluctantly consented to support the 1866 Reform Bill of the Russell-Gladstone Government as the best that could be hoped for in the circumstances, only to see it destroyed by a working alliance of Tories and renegade Whigs. When Russell and Gladstone thereupon resigned, and were succeeded by a Tory Government, led by Lord Derby and Disraeli, Bright decided that the time had come to unleash an agitation which should leave no Administration, Whig or Tory, any alternative to the acceptance of a really far-reaching Reform Bill. For this purpose Bright was willing to work both with the National Reform Union, which was enlisting middle-class support, and the National Reform League, which enrolled the working-class Radicals (No. 53). How Bright and his famous brother-Radical, John Stuart Mill, behaved at the height of the agitation of 1866–7 will be found spitefully but revealingly described by a Tory in No. 54, and Bright's sins, in Tory eyes, grew worse when, after Suffrage Extension on a large scale had been conceded, he " incited " further agitation on the Ballot (No. 55). The Sessions of 1867 and 1868 were in consequence devoted to a much more far-reaching Parliamentary Reform than either Whig or Tory had originally intended, and in December 1868 Bright was a Cabinet Minister of influence. A new political era had begun, and No. 56 shows Mill's speculations on the possibilities of the immediate future.

44 : *The Weekly Dispatch,* March 12, 1848

WITHOUT abating one tittle of the interest we feel for the great career of the revolution in France, we shall soon have no small part of our attention called to those effects which this stirring event will produce in other countries. Germany demands to be united, and to be free . . . The demands of the population everywhere are definite and alike. Perfect freedom and equality of religion, trial by jury, universal arming of the people, the right of public meetings, a free Press, and a re-presentation of the people in the Diet of Germany are the chief . . . In fact the people choose that Germany shall be a nation instead of a confederation of estates . . . The German Confederation, as the patriots must be blind not to see, has been a conspiracy of rulers against the people, each agreeing to support the other against Reform . . . If the nation is to be one . . . Ernest of Hanover may put by his crown for a curiosity, and must sink, with the whole lot of Coburgs and Mecklenburghs . . . into a German Peer . . . So magnificent a consummation as the political fusion of

Germany would be even a grander event than the regeneration of France . . . Such a final destruction of
the stupid, base and barbarous treaty of Vienna, would
indeed place the balance of Europe on a secure,
because national, foundation. The German and
Italian nations, each glorying in its independence,
would be a very different counterweight to any mad
ambition on the part of France, to the disjointed
proprietorship of slaves which Castlereagh, Metternich
and the other dealers in human flesh mapped out . . .
England must not be persuaded or cajoled into any
alliance with the old and bye-gone order of things . . .
We look with intense concern, with anxiety, but with
great hope to the future. A day or two will bring
decisive news from Italy . . .

45 : WILLIAM WILLIAMS : *An Address to the Electors
and Non-Electors of the United Kingdom on
the Defective State of the Representative System
and the consequent Unequal and Oppressive
Taxation and Prodigal Expenditure of the
Public Money,* 1849

THE National Parliamentary and Financial Reform
Association has been formed, whose principles are based
upon motions for Parliamentary Reform as proposed in
the House of Commons by Mr. Hume in the last two
Sessions, and supported by 84 members. These are

1st. Such an extension of the Franchise as will confer the right
to be registered as an Elector upon every man of full age,
not subject to any legal disability, who for 12 months
shall have occupied any tenement, or portion of a
tenement, for which he shall be rated, or shall have
claimed to be rated, to the relief of the poor.

2nd. The adoption of the system of voting by Ballot.

3rd. The limitation of the duration of Parliaments to three years.

4th. Such a change in the arrangement of the Electoral Districts as shall produce a more equal apportionment of Representatives to constituents.

5th. The abolition of the Property Qualification for Members of Parliament.

These principles have been submitted to great public meetings in all the Metropolitan Boroughs, and to 59 district meetings in those boroughs, and in all of them have been with acclamation unanimously sanctioned, as well as of great meetings in 25 large commercial and manufacturing towns in various parts of Great Britain . . . Its effects will be to increase the constituency from 1,061,000 to considerably more than 5,000,000 . . .

(Williams was a former Radical M.P. for Coventry.)

46: R. G. Gammage: *History of Chartism*

O'Connor, notwithstanding all his previous support of the middle-class (Reform) movement, now turned upon his new allies, and opposed the motion.

He would remind them of the deceit practised on the people in former times by the middle classes. The people had no more chance of getting justice from this class, than they had from the man in the moon. They must rely solely on themselves. The Financial Reformers would use them for their own purposes . . . we must not be considered puppets in the hands of the middle classes . . . He would tell them that although Cobden and Bright might now vote for the "Little Charter", if there was any chance of ever making that measure law, they would bribe some of their own party to prevent it. The aim of these men was to juggle for their own benefit. He told them, in conclusion, to place no confidence in any other class of the community but the working classes. For his own part, he would never confide nor co-operate with any other. He had spent upwards of £130,000 in their cause, and he would never desert them.

Clark showed that O'Connor had done more than any other man in the Chartist Association to aid the Parliamentary Reformers, and read extracts, shewing that he had, at an expense of £20, travelled nearly 600 miles to Aberdeen to attend one of their meetings . . . That he went to Norwich and supported them, had done so in his letters in the *Star* . . . and had strongly condemned all opposition. The reading of these extracts was a heavy blow to the supposed consistency of O'Connor . . .

(From R. G. Gammage's *History of Chartism* (1854). This contains the text of one of O'Connor's last addresses to the Manchester Conference of January 1851.)

47: *The Weekly Dispatch,* November 2, 1851

THE cause of despotism is the Cossack influence on the Continent. The oppression of the people, the treatment of realms as mere estates, and their people as serfs, and Royal properties, are the titles by which Russia rules beyond its own borders. It is this which makes almost every army in Europe . . . part of her forces. England has stood aside. Strong in her insular position, not believing in any wrong that can assail her, charged by commerce and manufactures with the interest of peace, she has regretfully but inactively suffered Muscovy to spread its filaments over all the other lands of Europe, and to dictate in France, in Naples and in Spain, as in Austria itself . . . It is not too much to say that Lord Palmerston, watching with a statesmanlike foresight and patriotic jealousy the encroachments of pure barbaric power . . . has not only been decried as a dangerous incendiary . . . but that the great commercial interests . . . have shrunk with a narrow-minded affright from the maintenance of our natural and rightful position in Europe, trembling at the chance of a war which the unanimous firmness of the nation would have repelled rather than invited . . . Then . . . the efforts of . . . the Peace Society have wonderfully tended to give courage to oppression . . . And again and again, treating of things in preference to names, have we had to assert . . . that the organized robbery and murder of Europe are not peace . . . This sluggish and, at no distant day, suicidal indifference might have gone on till this commonwealth had perished under it, but for the circumstances which Kossuth's arrival has called forth . . . It is not what Kossuth has said but what our American brethren have responded that has, at once, unmasked the honourable and natural remedy . . . The 25 millions of the free West are claiming to be placed in balance against the unwieldy serfdom of the East . . . Is there yet anything in France worthy to stand by the side of England and America in the struggle that must come? With what fervour we should welcome it! How proud would be the place of the three peoples, bidding with but a word, for that word would suffice, tyranny to lose its hold and retire! Or should we, indeed, see Frenchmen leagued with Cossacks . . . even that might be, but still the Anglo-Saxon people of the two hemispheres would set Italy, Hungary, Poland and Germany free . . .

48: William Rider: 1854

For 35 years I have belonged to the same school, and still believe it to be the bounden duty of every man to possess arms, and to learn their use; but while propounding this doctrine, I have invariably opposed partial and premature outbreaks, contending that a want of unity incapacitated us from compassing our object; and that we lacked this unity in consequence of man-worship, and the treachery and bickerings of self-constituted leaders, and idle adventurers. I repeat, that I still hold the same doctrine of man being armed and trained to enable him to cope with domestic enemy or foreign foe. I never thought your moral force, your ram's horns, or your silver trumpets would level the citadel of corruption. When I see a bold united people,

> With banners unfurled,
> Resolved for their freedom to die,

then, and then only, shall I have hope of my country's salvation. I glory in being of this good old school, and if on the brink of starvation, I would prefer the bullet of a physical force opponent, to the speech of a moral force comforter.

(R. G. Gammage's *History of Chartism*, p. 443)

49: Henry Brookes

The representation of the people, as it at present exists, is nothing but a hideous mockery. It is so by the usurpation and encroachments of the aristocracy and landed interests . . . It is surely no small matter, that by these usurpations the government of this, a great commercial country, is become the patrimony of two

153

rival factions of aristocratic families. Ruling absolute in their own House, and their brothers and sons, uncles and nephews, relatives and connections in the People's House, they are under no necessity to labour for the acquisition of that knowledge and experience which are essential . . . Yet they arrogate to themselves . . . all the highest offices and dignities whilst numbers of other men of talent and probity . . . are perpetually excluded . . . as " political adventurers ". All that either of these aristocratic factions require is, that a few of them should possess some tact and cleverness in debate . . . Even that necessity each faction occasionally ekes out by picking up and using as subservient tools men of intellect—not of their order . . .

And what have been the results of this monopoly of all power—legislative, civil and military? Have they not been abundantly manifest in bad commercial laws, badly administered; bad commercial treaties, nego-tiated by men trained in utter contempt of commercial pursuits . . . in the wars and rumours of wars for kingly and aristocratic institutions—never for the rights of peoples or the liberties of nations? . . . Taxes of every conceivable form and kind imposed upon trade and commerce . . . in ease of the landed interests? Has not that same interest for sixty years exempted itself from the payment of probate and legacy duty, inflicted stamp duties of enormous amount upon the small receipts, bills, notes, bonds, mortgages etc. required by the common people? . . .

Our diplomatic service has always been made the refuge of the destitute in intellect and purpose amongst the " families " and the appointments are consequently richly paid. No other country pays such extravagant salaries, and no other country is so ill-served . . .

For twenty or thirty years we have been talking of a national or general system of education for the people, of abolishing the odious Ecclesiastical Courts, and finding a substitute for church rates; of regulating the temporalities of the church by a series of ecclesiastical commissions, each of which has signally failed; of reforming the Court of Chancery, which is still unreformed . . .

Our bankruptcy laws . . . are the least efficient and the most oppressive and costly in Europe; our real property laws are still the most elaborately complicated, absurd and expensive in the world, and we are still without a general registry of title or deeds . . . There is positively no audit of the public expenditure . . .

Our civil expenditure is increasing by the million per annum . . . A million of money, at the least, has been sunk in shameful jobbery at the new Palace of Westminster, a costly but contemptible abortion . . . Prince Albert takes upon himself to appropriate £17,000 to Baron Marochetti for an English monument, it being his sovereign will and pleasure that English artists should not be allowed to compete for it . . .

If we want further illustrations of ignorance, incapacity and self-sufficiency . . . we have only to look at the events of the late war. With a ministry of sterling English character that war might doubtless have been avoided. When they and their system came to a dead lock, and the brave fellows who formed our sole hope . . . were dying by thousands, like discarded dogs in ditches . . . to my Lord Aberdeen the Order of the Garter.

The people saw but one man in all England fit to lead—and that one was Palmerston . . . Palmerston, if not a great man, was then our greatest ... If the other was a Cabinet of Lords, this was a Cabinet of more Lords: but it mattered little. The people's blood was up, money to any amount was poured into their hands ... the men who had to do the work got their heads at liberty ... and Palmerston " rode the high horse " ...

Then came the peace-parley—the test of his statesmanship—and showed the utter hollowness of his pretensions. When millions of money had been sown abroad—cast over Europe and Asia—when we might have said to Russia, "henceforth the shores of Asia and the shores of Circassia shall be free, you shall not repass the Caucasus ..." then our statesmen failed us. The court with its secret connections and paralyzing influences—the aristocracy in its mean subservience—our imperial ally were all for peace ...

The peace, which future historians will pronounce shameful, Lord Palmerston foresaw could be made to appear satisfactory, and that was enough for him ... Even those poor terms were made poorer still by gross ignorance and incapacity ... All Lord Palmerston's bluster about insisting upon the full performance of the treaty was mere bounce. Russia ... has given us in return a war in China, another in Persia, a massacre in Borneo, and a mutiny in our Indian army. This it is to have a government of emasculated courtiers and a subservient House of Commons ...

(Henry Brookes's *The Peers and the People, and the Coming Reform*, 1st edition, July 1857)

50: THE REFORM ASSOCIATION

List of the present House of Commons with the degree of its subjection to the House of Lords.

The well-known Parliamentarian, Roebuck, seems to have been mainly responsible for this programme.

OBJECT OF THE ASSOCIATION

To unite public opinion upon leading questions of Reform . . . knowledge on the following great public questions will be transmitted throughout the country.

I. *Administrative Reform*

1. Public Examination of all candidates for Public Employment.
2. Promotion by Merit, and Abolition of Patronage.
3. Publication in Detail of all National Expenditure.
4. Extension of Free Trade.
5. Direct Taxation (not Income Tax).
6. Simplification of procedure in all Law Courts.
7. Extension of Local Self-Government—Parochial and County.
8. Colonial Self-Government.
9. Open Diplomacy.
10. Prevention of Interference between Nations and their Governments. (Anti-Russian and pro-Turk.)

II. *Parliamentary Reform*

1. Extension of the Franchise.
2. Protection for the Voter.
3. Re-adjustment of Electoral Districts.
4. Shorter Parliaments.
5. Revision of the Qualification for English and Irish Members.
6. The same Electoral Laws for England, Ireland, Scotland and Wales.

51: JOHN BRIGHT: Speech at Manchester, December 10, 1858

BUT if you think it necessary that your members should be elected by some fair number of votes, that votes should be given with something like an equality of power, how far are you from this when you hear that 330 members of the House of Commons—more than one-half of the whole number—are returned by less than one-sixth even of that small number of persons to whom the franchise is entrusted? You give votes to a million out of six millions, and half the House of Commons is returned by less than 200,000 of those electors! And then, if bribery be somewhat common, and if intimidation, wherever it can be practised is almost universal, how can you come to the conclusion that there is any real freedom of election . . . ?

. . . Lord Derby, the present Prime Minister, . . . once gave us an illustration of what is understood in England by county representation. He said that, if anybody would tell him what were the politics of three or four of the great landed proprietors of any county, he could tell at once what were the politics of the Members for that county . . . the Members are the representatives of those great proprietors. They have . . . unfortunately for us, small sympathy with commerce, and they have never manifested, at least for the last sixty years, any sympathy whatever with Reform of any kind. How should they? They are connected with the peerage and the great territorial power. The members of their families, generally speaking, do not come into the operations of trade; they find employment—at least they find salaries—in the military or naval service, or some other service of the country; or they take shelter from the storms of life in some snug family living in the Church . . .

But we do not find fault only with the counties; the boroughs are not at all in a satisfactory state. I was looking down a list, the other night, beginning with the Tower Hamlets, the largest population, and coming down to . . . the smallest . . . I found that there were 71 boroughs, not one of which had a population of 10,000 persons . . . The whole population of the 71 boroughs is only 467,000, which is not very much more than the present population of Manchester and Salford; and yet these 71 boroughs return 117 Members to the House of Commons, while Manchester and Salford return only three members . . . These little boroughs are . . . very little better than what we used to describe by the unpleasant term of "rotten". . . . A very little clique . . . a neighbouring landowner—some subtle and not very scrupulous lawyer—by turning the "screw" can, if he likes, turn the scale . . . these boroughs . . . cannot pretend to the power of free election in any way whatsoever.

I come now to the result of all this—that a House of Commons so formed, becomes, for the most part . . . a sort of deputy to the House of Lords . . . It hates changes . . . It hates economy. The House hates equality of taxation. The succession-duty is a glaring instance of it. The income tax is another . . . It gives to property vast influence in the government of the country, and it perpetually shields property from its fair burden of taxation . . .

And now they do not give you the Ballot . . . Do you suppose there would be such a whip in the House, such a steady and powerful phalanx of Members brought up, County Members especially, to vote against the

Ballot, if they did not believe all we say in favour of the Ballot? You have had it discussed since the Reform Bill. The argument has been already exhausted for twenty years, yet for all that they do not give you the Ballot.

Take the question of Church Rates. A Bill to repeal the Church Rates has just passed the House of Commons . . . The arguments were the same before I went into the House of Commons that they were last session. Take the Game Laws. Would it be tolerated . . . by the people of this country, if they were fairly polled, that there should exist laws whose object is to promote, to the greatest possible extent, the preservation of wild animals for the sport of the territorial and wealthy classes? . . .

Then I come to the conclusion that Reform is necessary. But I can show you further that it is inevitable . . . The only great result of the Reform Bill, in the House, has been this, that it has introduced about one hundred men who do at times show some amount of independence, and they act free from the shackles of the Tory or Whig sections of the aristocracy. And it is we—it is by our work, it is by our speeches, by our votes, that we transfer the Government from one party to the other. But we make it impossible for either of them to conduct the Government upon those antiquated principles which we and the people of England are ready to abolish.

(The 1869 edition of Thorold Rogers's editions of Bright's *Speeches on Questions of Public Policy*)

52 : HENRY BROOKES

GREAT events have occurred since the first Edition of
this work in 1857. The terrible Indian Mutiny—the
infamous Conspiracy Bill—and the ignominious expulsion from power of Lord Palmerston . . . Never did
Ministry enjoy more power and popularity or abuse
them more . . .

The Derby Ministry, having abolished the property
qualification of members, have now presented their
" little Bill " on Parliamentary Reform for the people's
" acceptance ", but ere these lines are published, it will
probably have been " returned dishonoured ".

Who next? Lord John Russell or Sir James Graham?
Where is the " coming man "? Only one man stands
forth who seems to be the man for the time and the
occasion, and that one is JOHN BRIGHT. Mr. Bright may
not be everything a Radical party could desire, but he
has so many excellencies, and so few defects, that as
yet he stands alone, without a rival or competitor . . .

His claims to statesmanship are established beyond
all question, by the great and glorious success of his
free trade policy . . . No public man has exhibited
greater knowledge or more statesmanlike views of
India. Lord Canning's recent dispatch marvellously
corroborates Mr. Bright's recent speech; and every
mail from India is now proving that his policy alone
can preserve that Empire to us. These are claims which
the people can comprehend and appreciate, notwithstanding the cavils of noble lords and honourable
gentlemen, who seem to believe that statesmanship can
be found only within the charmed circle of certain
aristocratic families.

The attacks on the aristocracy with which he is reproached, were inevitable necessities: class government and class legislation constitute the case—the evils to be dealt with—they have destroyed the balance of the Constitution which he seeks to restore . . . He could not show what the people are entitled to demand, and ought to demand, without showing in what manner the Constitution has been encroached upon by the aristocracy . . .

His (Reform) measure is conceived in no party or class spirit: it is based on the same principles as the Reform Act of 1832 . . . and if it goes a little further than those principles which were carried out on 1832, it is still in the same direction and on the same road . . .

Let the people ask themselves have they any better man or any better measure to look to? . . . If not, they should rally round him . . . They must insist that the prescriptive rule which restricts all government offices to a few aristocratic families shall now be broken through, and that a few of the independent party in Parliament, with Mr. Bright at their head, shall be included in the next Administration, whoever may form it.

(The People's Edition (1859) of Henry Brookes's *The Peers and the People, and the Coming Reform*)

53A: THE NATIONAL REFORM UNION: *Statement*

In November 1861, the Leeds Working Men's Parliamentary Reform Association called a meeting of the Reformers of Yorkshire and Lancashire to consider the position of the Liberal Party. The gathering was a very successful one, though necessarily of a preliminary character. The result was the appointment of a Committee to take steps to convene a National Reform Conference, in London, in the following spring, to decide upon a Reform Platform. In May 1862, such a conference was held, and was attended by some of the more advanced Reform members of the House of Commons. A most animated debate took place . . . The issue of their deliberations was the adoption (with five dissentients) of the following resolution:

> That while the statements made in this Conference show the deep conviction of the people in favour of Manhood Suffrage, in which conviction a large proportion of the delegates fully sympathised, the Conference considers that the union of all classes of real Reformers is essential to the attainment of any real improvement of the representation, and with this view it submits to the country the following programme as a basis of action: Such an extension of the franchise as will confer the suffrage upon every male person, householder or lodger, rated or liable to be rated for the relief of the poor, together with a more equitable distribution of seats, vote by ballot, and a limitation of the duration of Parliament to three years.

An Executive Committee was appointed to prepare a Constitution . . . and to submit it to a National Conference, to be held in Manchester in the ensuing autumn.

Owing, however, to the Cotton crisis, it was impracticable to hold a meeting earlier than April 1864. On the 19th and 20th of that month a Conference took place in the Free Trade Hall, Manchester, when the Executive Committee presented their report . . . The new Society was designated the National Reform Union . . . It is now clear that the question of Parliamentary Reform has reached a crisis;

the Executive have therefore deemed it expedient to convene the present Conference to consider what steps can be taken at the next General Election . . .

(The National Reform Conference, May 15 and 16, 1865)

53B: THE NATIONAL REFORM LEAGUE

Manhood Suffrage and the Ballot

Fellow Countrymen, allow yourselves no longer to be deprived of these rights. Your brethren in Victoria, the Canadas, the great Republic of America, etc., enjoy them with benefit to their respective countries. Why not, then, the people of Great Britain and Ireland?

When the very moderate and honest measure of Reform, brought in by Mr. Gladstone last year, was not only rejected by its enemies, but scorn and insult were heaped upon the unenfranchised masses and their friends by the Tories, and also by a section of the so-called Liberal Party . . . your committee felt that it was only by combined and vigorous action, that any real measure of Reform could be wrung from the oligarchy, who have so long ruled this great empire.

The country has nobly responded to this call, and such a demand has been made by the united moral force of a great people, as to compel a reluctant and unwilling Government to pass a measure of Parliamentary Reform which, if not satisfactory to us, is at least much more extensive than we could have expected a short year ago . . .

The value of the present measure will depend greatly on the enlightened public opinion brought to bear . . . We shall again soon be called to agitate for the following measures:

164

I. The abolition of restrictions relative to the
   mode of paying rates upon which the
   franchise is based.
II. The equalization of the county and borough
   franchise.
III. A new and improved distribution of seats.
IV. The ballot, to protect the voter . . .
V. If not for annual, at least for triennial Parliaments . . .

(The League's Midland Department *Second Annual Report
and Balance Sheets from July* 1866 *to July* 1867)

54: FRANCIS HITCHMAN: *Public Life of the Earl of
Beaconsfield*

HOW THE " SECOND REFORM BILL " WAS FORCED ON BY
THE REFORM LEAGUE

THE Reform agitation had during the last few weeks
(July–August 1866) assumed alarming proportions. Mr.
Bright, Mr. Stuart Mill, and a handful of agitators,
mostly of the baser sort, devoted themselves to stirring
up the mob . . . and to clamouring with tremendous
energy against the Tory government . . . " Demonstrations "—vast meetings of working men with a choice
following of roughs and reprobates from the lowest
dens in London—were of weekly and almost of daily
occurrence. Sunday and week-day, wet weather or dry,
the unhappy residents in certain districts of the capital
were compelled to see vast mobs of the great unwashed
marching in procession to the discordant strains of
brass bands. Trafalgar Square was the favourite scene
of these performances. The first " demonstration " was
held there on the 2nd July, 1866. A few days later it
was announced that one was to be held in Hyde Park,
whereupon Sir Richard Mayne issued a prohibitory

notice . . . Mr. Mill . . . made an outrageous speech in the House upon the subject . . .

Despite the prohibition of Sir Richard Mayne . . . the mob, egged on by its leaders, and notably by Mr. Bright, whose wanton defiance of authority in this matter admits of neither excuse nor palliation, held its meeting in Hyde Park, knocked down the railings, trampled over the flower-beds, pelted the police . . . The meetings were not, indeed, intended as political gatherings. They were, by the frank admission of Mr. Mill himself, intended to overawe the Government . . . It is melancholy to recall the distracted circumstances of that distracted time and the infinite follies of the advocates of change. . . . Thus, on the 8th of August a Reform Meeting was held in the Guildhall, presided over by the Lord Mayor, and attended by the delegates of the Reform League. All the speakers were working men, and the meeting pledged itself to manhood suffrage and the Ballot. Three weeks later a demonstration was held at Birmingham, attended, it was said, by a quarter of a million people, at which Mr. Bright held Mr. Lowe up to popular execration—a performance which he repeated a month later at Manchester, adding to his former vituperation a personal attack on Lord Derby . . .

The most remarkable of all the displays were, however, one in which Mr. Bright figured at Glasgow and a "demonstration" in London. At the Glasgow gathering, Mr. Bright who . . . had drawn down upon himself a severe . . . rebuke from Mr. Disraeli, on account of his habitually depreciatory way of speaking of the House of Commons . . . chose to declare that that assembly was utterly unworthy of popular confidence. "If the clerk of the House," said he, "were placed at

Temple Bar, and had orders to lay his hand on the shoulder of every well-dressed and apparently clean-washed man who passed through the ancient bar until he numbered 658, and if the Crown summoned those 658 men . . . , my honest conviction is that you would have a better Parliament than now exists." The other was a grotesque gathering got up by the London Trades Unions, who marched in procession from the parade ground at Whitehall to Chiswick, in order to listen to the oratory of a conceited glassblower named Leicester, who, after denouncing the House of Commons as a " set of little-minded, decrepit, hump-backed, one-eyed scoundrels ", asked, " What had Lord Derby done? ", and answered himself : —" He has translated Homer. But he could not make one of those beautiful specimens of glass-work which had been carried in procession that day . . . There was not a stocking-weaver in Leicester or clodhopper in the kingdom rendering service to the State who was not quite as useful as Lord Derby " . . .

Trash of this kind . . . was poured out in abundance during the whole of the autumn and winter. What made it noticeable was that men like Mr. Stuart Mill and Mr. Gladstone . . . were not ashamed to encourage the agitation, and to point to it as a reason for con-ceding "a large and comprehensive measure" of Reform. It is true that both professed to disclaim all connection with the League, but both supported its demands in the House of Commons, and used its demonstrations as arguments in favour of their views . . . Mr. Stuart Mill, for example, was one of the most furious partisans of the period . . .

(A hostile Tory account of the Radical agitation to carry the Second Reform Bill, passed by Disraeli (2nd edition, 1881, p. 378 et sqq.).)

55: JOHN BRIGHT: Letter to the President of the Reform League

BRIGHT REQUESTS THE "AGITATORS" TO
CONTINUE

August 18, 1867

MY DEAR MR. BEALES,—I am glad to see that it is not intended to discontinue the organization and labours of the Reform League, although so great a step has been gained in the extension of the suffrage. On that branch of the question of Reform I presume you will not feel it necessary now to agitate further, so far as the boroughs are concerned. But . . . the more wide the suffrage, the more there are of men in humble circumstances who are admitted to the exercise of political rights, the more clearly is it necessary that the shelter of the ballot should be granted. I am confident it would lessen expenses at elections, greatly diminish corruption, and destroy the odious system of intimidation which now so extensively prevails . . . I hope all our friends throughout the country will accept the ballot as the next great question for which, in connection with Parliamentary Reform, they ought to contend. Without this safeguard there can be no escape from corruption and oppression at elections, and our political contests will still remain what they now are, a discredit to us as a free and intelligent people.

If the Reform League and Reform Union will make the ballot their next work, they must soon succeed. I need not tell you that I shall heartily join in their labours for this great end . . .

(The Reform League claimed 430 branches and had been chiefly responsible for the large-scale working-class agitation to carry the 1867 Reform Act. (*The Public Letters of John Bright*, pp. 135–6.))

56: J. S. MILL: Speech to his Constituents, July 22, 1868

MR. J. S. MILL on rising was received with loud cheers, which were long continued. The hon. gentleman said . . .

I will deal chiefly with the future . . . The nation has now, to a considerable extent a new task before it . . . There are two kinds of improvements: one kind, which to enable them to be accomplished, only requires that the nation should make up their mind that it shall be done . . . The Irish Church, when the nation has determined, as I believe it has determined [Loud applause] that it shall no longer commit the great injustice of endowing with the national property the Church of a small minority . . . it has only to make known its determination . . . But the statesmanship of the country has much more to do nowadays than merely to abolish bad institutions. It has to make good laws for a state of society which never existed in the world before . . . a vast manufacturing and commercial industry has thrown itself up . . . and from the necessities of the case, a hundred evils have sprung up along with it . . . There are now many things to be done which demand long and patient thought . . . For instance, let us take the question which is in every one's mind at present—the proper relations between capital and labour . . . how far has the public mind advanced on the subject? It has got thus far: that the old relation between workmen and employers is out of joint . . .

Next let me speak of our pauperism and of our system of poor relief. We know the vices of the system. We know that vast sums are levied, and that those who most deserve and most need public charity are badly relieved. We know that the nursing of the sick, the care of the aged and the helpless, the education of the young, are often . . . a cruel mockery [Loud cheers] . . . What is wanted is to put into the important positions men of organizing minds . . . who know how to give due and adequate relief to destitution without encouraging those to claim who can do without it. Then as to the state of our town population. The poorer quarters of our great cities are nests of disease and vice for want of proper sanitary arrangements, and from the bad construction and wretched overcrowding of the dwellings of the poor [Applause]. How are these things to be remedied . . . It is a matter for thought and study, and one which will tax to the utmost the highest legislative and administrative ability. Next, as to education. We are all determined that a good education the people shall have, cost what it may [Loud applause] . . . Now turn to the great subject of administrative reform. We might have our persons and property far better protected than at present, paying much less for protection, but paying to competent persons for good service what is now jobbed away or wasted. We might have a defensive force much more effective than at present, for a fraction of what our navy and army cost us; but it requires men with planning heads, organizing and contriving minds . . .

(*Addresses of the Hon. R. W. Grosvenor and J. S. Mill Esq., at a Public Meeting of their Constituents . . . on the 22nd July,* 1868)

PART VI

FROM THE SECOND TO THE THIRD REFORM BILL

1867—1884

FROM THE SECOND TO THE THIRD
REFORM BILL
1867—1884

INEVITABLY, the Reform Bill of 1867, which still contained a number of precautions against " excessive " democracy, was found unsatisfactory in practice. The Election Address issued in 1868 by Samuel Morley, one of Bright's leading Parliamentary friends (No. 57A), called for the abolition of the Bill's "vexatious and useless ratepaying clauses", the introduction of Vote by Ballot and a much wider redistribution of seats, and the same demands may be found in the second and " extremer " Radical Election Address of 1868, reprinted as No. 57B. Such demands, together with criticism of the unsatisfactory state of the franchise in the Counties, became part of the political stock-in-trade, even of moderate Radicals, as did the various Dissenting grievances which occupied so large a share in the politics of ensuing years. Morley, who was himself a leading representative of Dissenting grievances, hinted in his Address at a readiness to undertake the Disestablishment of the State Churches of the United Kingdom; and the abolition of compulsory Church rates in England was, in fact, carried through during the course of 1868. The abolition of Church privileges, however, at the Universities and at the endowed schools of the country was a thornier problem, and though decisions between 1867 and 1885 moved generally in the Radical direction, it was only at the price of constant compromise with the House of Lords.

On elementary education, the " secular " solution, advocated by Morley and the Radical Dissenters, was the prelude to a long and bitter struggle, begun in 1870 and hardly ended to-day. One of the great Radical grievances from 1870 onwards was the " over-generous " financial support offered to " sectarian schools " under the Liberal Education Act of 1870 and subsequent Acts. When, in 1902, a Conservative Government ventured to put the " sectarian school " on the rates as well as on the taxes, there was a Radical and Dissenting revolt whose consequences were hardly over by 1914.

On Church Disestablishment the Radicals succeeded in the very exceptional Irish case in 1869, but their next success, on Welsh Disestablishment, was fated to be delayed until 1914. No. 57A illustrates the Radical campaign against the House of Lords that had to be undertaken before Irish Church Disestablishment was enacted in 1869. Following it, as 58B, is Joseph Chamberlain's declaration on Republicanism, made in December 1872 and typical of the attitude which " advanced Radicals " permitted themselves on the question of the Crown. No. 58c completes the picture of the main interests of the " advanced " during the period 1868–74 by showing how the Newcastle Radical M.P., Joseph Cowen, was preparing, in 1874, to " get up steam " in the North for a third Reform Bill.

The country was, however, fated to have six years of " Beaconsfieldism " from 1874 to 1880, and much Radical energy, during the period, was consumed in protesting against Beaconsfield's courses in foreign and Imperial policy (No. 59). In domestic politics one of the most significant and important manifestations of the period was the appearance of an increasing number of working-class Radical Clubs, especially in the London area, and the vigour of their Reform demands may be judged from the Southwark Radical Club's Election Manifesto of 1880 (No. 60). The more normal Radical Election Address of 1880 (No. 61) tended to make the main issue one of foreign policy, and the reversal of " Beaconsfieldism " abroad and in the Empire was naturally one of the chief Radical concerns for years after Beaconsfield's ejection. Yet something was done for the Dissenters in the Burials Bill of 1880, and a great blow against the worst aspects of " landlordism " was struck in the famous Irish Land Act of 1881. Finally, in 1883, despite Irish difficulties which were growing steadily more trying and dangerous, the Radicals, under the leadership of Chamberlain and Dilke, resolved to force the pace and to secure the most far-reaching Parliamentary Reform that had ever been undertaken in Britain. No. 62 shows how the new move forward was engineered.

Across the Atlantic, meanwhile, there had appeared in Henry George's *Progress and Poverty* of 1879 an eloquent denunciation of " landlordism " as the main scourge of the Old World and the main threat to the happiness of the New. By 1883 the book had won its way extensively in Britain (No. 63), and for years afterwards the impression it made on all the " advanced thought " of the country was profound. From the Joseph Chamberlain of 1885, indeed, to the Lloyd George of 1909, and even of 1929, echoes from the anti-landlordism of *Progress and Poverty* were continuous. Although Socialists ultimately ridiculed the spectacle of wealthy " monopoly capitalists ", politically disguised as " advanced Radicals ", leading the denunciation of

175

"land monopoly", there can be no doubt that Socialism, too, gained a great impetus from the appearance and influence of *Progress and Poverty*. Such declarations of the perfect Radical faith as Labouchere gave to his Northampton constituents in 1885 (No. 64) certainly tended to look old-fashioned by the 1890s, and so did those of the " working-man " Radical, George Howell, at Bethnal Green (No. 65).

57A: SAMUEL MORLEY: Election Address at Bristol, 1868

I ACCEPT the Reform Bill of 1867 as a wise concession of the franchise to large numbers of our fellow-countrymen, from whom it had been too long withheld, and I do not so distrust the character of Englishmen as to fear that they will employ their newly acquired privileges for selfish and unworthy purposes. I desire to abolish the vexatious and useless ratepaying clauses, to obtain an enlarged scheme of redistribution of seats in correspondence with the just demands of our population; and now, more than ever, to prevent the intimidation and corruption of the electors by the protection of the ballot.

I am in favour of entire freedom in religious conviction and worship. I believe that dependence on the State is a source of weakness to religious men, and a hindrance and obstruction to their efforts . . . The abolition of compulsory Church rates, and the complete opening to the entire nation of all endowments, which can be proved to be national, in connection with our universities and public schools, are measures that I would heartily support.

On the subject of education, it appears necessary that our present system should be supplemented, especially in certain districts, by the establishment of schools, in which secular instruction should be given; and, without resort to compulsion, increased facilities and inducements be presented for the education of the children of the poorest and neglected classes. . . .

(Morley was elected and sat in Parliament from 1868 to 1886. (Edwin Hodder, *Life of Samuel Morley*, 1887, pp. 257-8))

57B: J. Passmore Edwards: Election Address at Truro, 1868

More "extreme" Radicalism

I would repeal the ratepaying clauses of the last Reform Bill: I would place the means of education within the reach of every child in the Kingdom: I am in favour of the Ballot and an equalised distribution of Parliamentary constituencies: I would insist on a wise economy in every department of the State: I would endeavour to apply the teachings of Cobden, and cultivate a policy of non-intervention and, wherever possible, substitute arbitration for war in the settlement of national disputes: I would abolish the purchase system in the army: I would put an end to the game laws: I would make the privileges of our national universities accessible to men of every religious creed: I would do my best to make the colonies self-supporting: I would abolish death punishments and I would vote for an equalisation of the poor law and a more useful administration of charitable endowments.

There are other social questions which would claim my attention such as improved dwellings for the working classes, . . . the protection of the funds of all legally constituted trade societies, and the cultivation of waste lands and revision of the licensing system.

58A: JOSEPH CHAMBERLAIN: Speech at the Birmingham Town Hall, June 15, 1869

IT is scarcely likely that we shall sit tamely by and see our efforts frustrated by the obstinacy or bigotry of one hundred or two hundred persons, however highly placed they may be. The majority in the Commons of 114 represents the wishes of 6,000,000 people. The 60 Peers opposed to them in the Lords represent three things. Some of them represent the oppression of Feudal lords in times gone by . . . In the second place, some of them represent the great wealth acquired by the possession of land in the vicinity of large towns— e.g. Manchester and Birmingham—which land enriched its proprietors without care or labour on their part. And lastly, they represent, and very imperfectly, too, in many cases, the brains, the intelligence, and the acquirements of ancestors long since dead, who unfortunately have been unable to transmit to their descendants the talents by which they rose . . . I venture to hope that the effect of this and similar meetings will be that the House of Lords will be advised in time, . . . and avert, for this time at least, the spectacle of a conflict between the Peers and the People.

(Chamberlain was speaking on the Peers and Irish Church Disestablishment. (S. H. Jeyes, *Mr. Chamberlain,* 1903))

58B: JOSEPH CHAMBERLAIN, 1872

I HAVE been taxed with professing Republicanism. I hold, and very few intelligent men do not now hold, that the best form of Government for a free and enlightened people is that of a Republic, and that is a form of Government to which the nations of Europe are surely and not very slowly tending. But, at the same time, I am not at all prepared to enter into an agitation to upset the existing state of things, to destroy Monarchy, and to change the name of the titular Ruler of this country. I do not consider that name a matter of the slightest importance. What is of real importance is the spread of a real Republican spirit among the people. The idea, to my mind, that underlies Republicanism is this: that in all cases merit should have a fair chance, that it should not be handicapped in the race by any accident of birth or privilege; that all men should have equal rights before the Law, equal chances of serving their country . . .

58C: JOSEPH COWEN, 1874

NORTHERN REFORM LEAGUE

OBJECTS

To assist in creating such an expression of public opinion as will necessitate the passing of a measure of electoral reform based on universal suffrage, triennial Parliaments, and payment of members; and that will secure a better apportionment of representatives to population, an extension of the time for polling, and the payment of all necessary election expenses by the ratepayers.

Joseph Cowen Esq., M.P., *President*.

Vice-Presidents:

Dr. Rutherford, Newcastle; Thomas Burt, M.P., Newcastle; James Birkett, Byker; John Lucas, Gateshead; Robert Elliott, Choppington Colliery; Dr. James Trotter, Bedlington; William Crawford, Durham.

The co-operation of all Liberals is respectfully invited by the Executive of the Northern Reform League, the aim of which is the propagation of Political Reform, and assisting in the returning of advanced Liberals to Parliament. The League already numbers upwards of 57,000 members.

YEARLY SUBSCRIPTION, NOT LESS THAN 1*s*.

(Joseph Cowen, the Radical M.P. for Newcastle, wrote this for a Northern Reform League pamphlet.)

59: JOHN BRIGHT: Speech at Manchester, October 25, 1879

THEY passed a Bill . . . the Public Worship Regulation Bill . . . They thought it was a popular measure . . . Well, the result of it has been this . . . that it has not in the slightest degree, I believe, succeeded in putting down Ritualism . . .

Mr. Cross . . . I think was boastful of the character and the expected services of the Artisans' Dwellings

Bill . . . It was a very sensible Bill, but it was in no sense an Artisans' Dwellings Bill, and I am not sure that a single score of artisans, or that a single one artisan is now in a comfortable and cleanly and wholesome house in consequence of the passing of that Bill, other than he would have been if that Bill had never been heard of . . .

Last year they were brought within an inch of war with Russia. This year you have had two wars—one in Africa and one in Asia. You recollect the strain that was put upon the Government here to furnish troops to put down a savage chief in South Africa. The King of the Zulus had few or no rifles, he had no artillery: he had no horses, and therefore no cavalry, and yet to put down this King, to disperse his troops, to take him prisoner, put a strain on our military resources . . . Well, but what do you think of a Government that had this difficulty with King Cetewayo, what do you think of this Government only 18 months ago within a hair's breadth of going into a sanguinary and destructive war with the Emperor of a country that could call under his banners at one time not less than 700,000 or 800,000 men? [Cheers]. And yet, Sir, there were criminals at headquarters [Loud cheers] and there were fools and imbeciles among the people [Laughter and cheers] and there was baseness among the proprietors and the writers of our newspapers [Loud cheers]—there was all this to give, for a time, a semblance of popularity to a madness and to a guilt such as I have described [Hear, hear]. If the Zulu war had been brought before the House of Commons: if the Afghan war with its fraud and its slaughter and its chaos over that region had been brought before the House of Commons: if it had been submitted to the

House of Commons that we had to go to war with Russia upon this simple question—whether Bulgaria should all be free or whether a part of it should be free and a portion less free— . . . does any man here believe that the Tory party themselves would have, by distinct vote in the House of Commons, plunged the country into any one of these wars? [No and cheers] . . .

We have heard lately a great deal of "Imperial policy" and of a "great empire". These are phrases which catch the ignorant and unwary [Hear, hear]. Since this Government came into office your great empire—upon the map—has grown much greater. They have annexed the islands of Fiji [Laughter] : they have annexed also the country of the Transvaal, in South Africa, which is said to be as large as France. They have practically annexed the land of the Zulus and they have practically annexed Afghanistan. They have added also to your dominions the island of Cyprus in the Mediterranean [Much laughter], and they have incurred enormous, incalculable responsibilities in Egypt and Asia Minor. All these add to the burdens . . . of the 34,000,000 people who inhabit Great Britain and Ireland. We take the burden and we pay the charge. This policy may lend a seeming glory to the Crown, and may give scope for patronage and promotion, and pay and pensions to a limited and favoured class, but to you, the people, it brings expenditure of blood and treasure, increased debt and taxes, and added risks of war in every quarter of the globe.

(*The Approaching General Election, Speeches of the Marquis of Hartington and John Bright, delivered at Manchester on October 24 and 25, 1879*)

60: GEORGE SHIPTON: Declaration of his Candidature, 1880

WEALTHY men, professing popular opinions, have been trusted over and over again; but after obtaining national notoriety, they have deserted the cause of the people, and in the sunshine of place and emolument have ripened into obstructives and poor imitations of Conservatives. To prevent this repeated disappointment of the people I . . . would urge with all my power the speedy adoption, among others, of the following measures:

1. Reform of the Land Laws.

2. A thoroughly representative municipal government for the whole Metropolis which would save the ratepayers two millions per annum.

3. Revision of the prerogatives of the Crown.

4. Disestablishment and Disendowment of the English Church which would give about ten millions annually to provide a Free Education for the People.

5. Self-Government for Ireland.

6. Reform of the Magistracy and Jury Laws.

7. Triennial Parliaments and an extension of Polling Hours . . . from 8 a.m. to 10 p.m.

8. Compulsory establishment of School Boards in all districts with compulsory, gratuitous, and secular instruction.

9. Complete and effectual reform of the City Guilds.

10. Candidates to be relieved of official election expenses, and such election expenses to be officially audited.

11. A thorough revision and ultimate abolition of the pension list.

183

12. Compulsory registration by local officials of voters for Parliamentary, School Board and Municipal elections.

13. Equal electoral voting power.

14. Registered resident suffrage.

15. The abolition of property or rating qualification for parochial and municipal offices.

16. An equitable rating of all property for the purposes of local taxation and a national equalisation of the poor and education rates.

17. Abolition of the only purely hereditary Chamber in Europe, the House of Lords.

(Shipton was the candidate of the Southwark Radical Club and stood as a working-class Radical.)

61: W. S. CAINE: Election Address at Scarborough, 1880

THE Conservative policy was unchanged: agitation and disturbance abroad to divert attention from needful reforms at home. When Mr. Disraeli took office in 1874 he informed Parliament that the relations of England with every European Power were on a perfectly friendly footing. Now we find ourselves estranged from all the rising nationalities of Eastern Europe, whom we have driven into the arms of ambitious and despotic Russia. We have made treaties with our vaunted ally Turkey, to be scorned by its rotten government to the point of broken diplomatic relations. France is uneasy and suspicious about Egypt. Greece feels herself cheated by the English of her legitimate frontier rectifications. In Asia we were at war with Afghanistan. In Africa we had effected the ill-considered annexation of the

184

Transvaal. Sir Bartle Frere would never have embarked upon a cruel and unjust (Zulu) war but from the encouragement he had received from the high-handed Imperialism of his chief at home.

Turning to domestic legislation, Mr. Caine found it was chiefly abortive or retrogressive. Their Artisans' Dwellings Act is virtually a dead letter, and its powers have not been applied in half-a-dozen towns in the kingdom. Their Licensing Act, their Elementary Education Act, their Royal Titles Act, and their Endowed Schools Act were reactionary and mischievous. The Agricultural Holdings Act was a confessed failure as an attempt to remedy a deep-seated grievance . . .

The definite proposals of legislation to which he committed himself were: (1) the equalisation of the voting qualification of ratepayers, (2) religious equality, (3) the Burials Bill, (4) the reform of the Land and Game Laws, (5) Sunday closing of public-houses and reform of the Licensing Laws, (6) self-government for country districts, (7) abolition of flogging in the Army and Navy, (8) repeal of the Contagious Diseases Acts, (9) retrenchment.

(W. S. Caine was one of the successful candidates at the 1880 General Election. (*W. S. Caine, M.P., A Biography*, by John Newton, 1907))

62: H. JEPHSON: *The Platform*

IN May 1883 a meeting was held in London of the National Liberal Federation, and a resolution passed urging the Government to introduce a Bill extending the franchise to householders in counties. It was then resolved that . . . a conference . . . should be called.

Accordingly such a conference was called, and met at Leeds on the 17th October, 1883 . . . Mr. J. Morley presided . . . "The present Conference," he said, "was a proof of the conviction which was growing in the Radical party, that it was not enough for them to be the helpless exponents of excellent ideas, but that they must organise, they must unite . . . Their starting-point was that reform was necessary; their discussion was to be as to procedure and details."

After considerable discussion as to the question of the precedence of Parliamentary Reform, London Government Reform, and Local Government Reform, it was decided . . . to give the precedence to Parliamentary Reform . . .

A resolution was also carried that a franchise Bill having been passed, a measure should follow for the redistribution of seats, such as would give as nearly as possible an equal value to every vote, and secure a true expression of the will of the nation . . .

On the 29th February, 1884, Mr. Gladstone moved in the House of Commons for leave to introduce a Bill assimilating the county and borough franchise, or, in other words, extending the franchise to every householder in counties. The measure proposed would, it was estimated, add 2,000,000 of voters to the electoral body. A measure for the redistribution of seats would follow the next session. The Bill passed the House of Commons by large majorities. In the House of Lords, however, the Bill was, on the 8th July, what some called "hung up", others "rejected", by the adoption of a resolution not to assent to its second reading until their Lordships had knowledge of the Government scheme of the redistribution of seats. . . .

Instantly, on the rejection of the Bill by the Lords, the Platform was appealed to . . . The Platform led off with a great reform demonstration in Hyde Park on the 21st of July . . . A huge procession of some 25,000 to 30,000, which took three hours to pass a given point, marched through the streets of London to Hyde Park. There were representatives from endless numbers of political and trades organisations, and clubs, and associations; there were banners innumerable, and numerous bands of music . . . The streets were crowded with spectators. The procession was not barred out of Hyde Park as in 1866, but was given unrestricted admission. Tens of thousands had assembled in the Park, and seven platforms had been constructed for the speakers. One identical resolution was proposed at all of them . . .

A great Conservative demonstration was held at Sheffield on the 22nd July. Here Lord Salisbury spoke . . . " The House of Commons was elected upon issues that have passed away; its life has been nearly spent; it is the most servile House of Commons— servile to the Minister, servile to the caucus—that the Palace of Westminster has ever seen; and we are denounced because we will not allow this House of Commons, so discredited—discredited by every circumstance, discredited by every by-election . . . to settle upon an unsound, partisan, and inequitable basis the Constitution which we are appointed to protect.

"The Government set up all sorts of shams and counterfeits; they descend into the streets; they call for processions; they imagine that 30,000 radicals going to amuse themselves in London on a given day

187

expresses the public opinion of the country . . .
Nothing can have been more good-humoured as yet
than the multitudes of their own partisans whom they
have summoned into the streets to keep them in
countenance. But they appeal to the streets . . . that
has its dangerous side . . . We at all events will not
consent to be guided by the public opinion of the
streets " . . .

The effect of the agitation is known to all. Within
less than two months the Franchise Bill became law,
and in the following session the almost greater measure
was passed for the redistribution of seats. The one
added over 2,000,000 of voters to the electoral body;
the other practically realised one of the " six points "
which had been demanded by the Charter—equal
electoral districts.

(Jephson describes the tactics of the agitation for the Third
Reform Bill of 1884. (Op. cit., 1892, ii, p. 256 et sqq.))

63 : HENRY GEORGE : *Progress and Poverty*

OUR boasted freedom necessarily involves slavery, so
long as we recognize private property in land. Until
that is abolished, Declarations of Independence and
Acts of Emancipation are in vain. So long as one man
can claim the exclusive ownership of the land from
which other men must live, slavery will exist, and as
material progress goes on, must grow and deepen! . . .

Mr. Mill's plan for nationalizing the future
" unearned increase in the value of land " by fixing the
present market value of all lands and appropriating
to the state future increase of value, would not add to

the injustice of the present distribution of wealth, but it would not remedy it . . .

Herbert Spencer says: "Had we to deal with the parties who originally robbed the human race of its heritage, we might make short work of the matter." Why not make short work of the matter anyhow? For this robbery is not like the robbery of a horse or a sum of money, that ceases with the act. It is a fresh and continuous robbery, that goes on every day and every hour. It is not from the produce of the past that rent is drawn; it is from the produce of the present. It is a toll levied upon labour constantly and continuously. Every blow of the hammer, every stroke of the pick, every thrust of the shuttle, every throb of the steam engine pay it tribute. It levies upon the earnings of the men who, deep underground, risk their lives . . . it claims the just reward of the capitalist and the fruits of the inventor's patient effort . . . it robs the shivering of warmth; the hungry, of food; the sick, of medicine; the anxious, of peace . . . It crowds families of eight and ten into a single squalid room . . .

It is not merely a robbery in the past; it is a robbery in the present—a robbery that deprives of their birthright the infants that are now coming into the world! Why should we hesitate about making short work of such a system? Because I was robbed yesterday, and the day before, and the day before that, is it any reason that I should suffer myself to be robbed to-day and to-morrow? any reason that I should conclude that the robber has acquired a vested right to rob me? . . .

What more than anything else prevents the realisation of the essential injustice of private property in land . . . is that mental habit which makes anything that has long existed seem natural and necessary . . .

If it were true that land had always been treated as private property, that would not prove the justice or necessity of continuing so to treat it . . . but . . . this is *not* true. On the contrary, the common right to land has everywhere been primarily recognized, and private ownership has nowhere grown up save as the result of usurpation. Historically, as ethically, private property in land is robbery. It nowhere springs from contract; it can nowhere be traced to perceptions of justice or expediency; it has everywhere had its birth in war and conquest, and in the selfish use which the cunning have made of superstition and law. . . .

This is clear—that in Great Britain to-day the right of the people as a whole to the soil of their native country is much less fully acknowledged than it was in feudal times. A much smaller proportion of the people own the soil, and their ownership is much more absolute. The commons . . . have, all but a small remnant of yet worthless land, been appropriated to individual ownership and inclosed; the great estates of the church . . . have been diverted from that trust to enrich individuals; the dues of the military tenants have been shaken off, and the cost of maintaining the military establishment and paying the interest upon an immense debt accumulated by wars has been saddled upon the whole people . . . The crown lands have mostly passed into private possession, and for the support of the royal family and all the petty princelings who marry into it, the British workman must pay in the price of his mug of beer and pipe of tobacco. The English yeoman—the sturdy breed who won Crécy, and Poictiers, and Agincourt—are as extinct as the mastodon. The Scottish clansman, whose right to the soil of his native hills was then as undisputed as that of his chieftain, has been driven out to make room for the sheep ranges or deerparks of that chieftain's descendant; the tribal right of the Irishman has been turned into a tenancy-at-will. Thirty thousand men have legal power to expel the whole population from five-sixths of the British Islands, and the vast majority of the British people have no right whatsoever to their native land save to walk the streets or trudge the roads . . .

(This extract is taken from the English edition of 1883.)

64: HENRY LABOUCHERE: Election Address at Northampton, 1885

I BELONG to the party of progress. I am in favour of the abolition of a hereditary Upper Chamber; of the disendowment and disestablishment of the State Church; of Free Education; of local self-government based upon those only possessing power who have been elected to exercise it; of a drastic and radical reform of our Land Laws; of such alteration in our system of taxation as will secure equality of sacrifice; of shorter Parliaments; of the payment of Members; and of the full recognition of the principle that, when a duly qualified citizen has been elected by a constituency to represent it in Parliament, his right to sit and legislate is absolute. I am opposed to further Royal Grants; to sums of money being voted to generals and admirals; to sinecures, to perpetual pensions, and to all other such abuses. I would give to Ireland the fullest measure of Home Rule, consistent with the integrity of the Empire. I view with distrust and disapproval all schemes for the extension of the Empire, and object to British blood and treasure being expended in foreign matters which do not concern us; my conviction being that, if we do not meddle with other nations, other nations will think twice before meddling with us. I would have army and navy strong for defence, but not for defiance, and I desire to see promotion in both dependent upon merit rather than birth or favour. In the Civil Service I would have the humbler members adequately paid, but I think that economy may be advantageously practised in regard to the salaries of some of the higher officials. I shall support any Administration which represents the opinions of the party to which I belong; but I shall not hesitate to raise my voice in protest should any Administration . . . lag on the path of progress . . . or waste the national resources . . .

65: GEORGE HOWELLS: Election Address at Bethnal Green, 1885

"THE Ballot Act being only as yet a temporary measure, I would amend it where required, and make it a permanent statutory law. I am also in favour of triennial Parliaments . . .

"As a fervent believer in representative government, I am opposed to the existence of an hereditary House of Peers. The House of Lords is non-representative and irresponsible. It represents class interest and promotes class-legislation. It is the embodiment of a caste and of privileges. It has resisted all measures of reform as long as it dared . . . The members of the peerage, their families and relatives have for generations monopolised place, power, privileges, pay and pensions. Within a period of 35 years, some 350 peers, with their families and relatives, numbering 8,523 persons, have held 13,880 offices and have drawn as salaries and pensions £108,614,632 from the revenues of the country, and this too, while thousands have been in a starving condition from want of employment and food. And be it remembered, these recipients of state pay never pay their full share of taxation according to their means . . .

" I am strongly opposed to hereditary pensions, and also to expenditure on royal palaces, yachts and retainers, the latter being mere courtiers, basking in the presence of royalty, and reclining in indolence under the shadow of the court, draw their annual salaries as if for useful work . . ."

Mr. Howell is altogether opposed to the present union of the Church and State. He desires " a thorough reform of the land laws, the abolition of primogeniture and entail and of all settlements tying up land and preventing its free sale, and of the entire sweeping away of the game laws "; also " the enfranchisement of lease-hold and the cultivation of waste lands, so as to give employment to surplus labour, and at the same time to increase the quantity of home-grown food for the people."

" I am in favour," he further tells us, " of a large and comprehensive measure of local self-government, based upon popular suffrage and representation according to population . . ." As regards London government, he is anxious to secure " one undivided municipal authority for the whole metropolis, elected by popular suffrage . . . special care being taken to secure the rightful application of the London guilds and churches."

" I am in favour of retrenchment as well as reform,"

says Mr. Howell. "Our national expenditure is enormous and excessive, and yet we are told by 'experts' that the country is in a defenceless state. A large increase of military and naval expenditure is now taking place—the result of panic and Jingo bluster and defiance." But he had faith in the democracy, and believes that, when we have obtained a truly representative system of government . . . we shall hear of no more such crimes as the bombardment of Alexandria, or consequent blunders like the war in the Soudan.

(The *Weekly Dispatch* of June 7, 1885, reports the programme on which George Howell began nearly ten years in Parliament as M.P. for North-East Bethnal Green.)

PART VII

RADICALISM "SOCIALISED"

1885-1914

RADICALISM "SOCIALISED"

1885–1914

LONG before the *Radical Programme* of 1885 was issued as a pamphlet, reproducing some of the writing Chamberlain and Morley had already done for the *Fortnightly Review*, there had been Radical candidates, capable (as No. 57B shows) of putting considerable morsels of Socialism into their policies. But it was Chamberlain who, in 1884 and 1885, really took Radicalism forward to a platform for which (as Document 66 makes clear) the French name of Radical-Socialism would not have been inappropriate. Chamberlain, of course, dreamed of putting his Radical Socialism into effect through a powerful Radical wing in a Gladstonian Cabinet. But the fatal Home Rule split of 1886 came just when the first fruits of the *Radical Programme* seemed about to be reaped (No. 67), and Chamberlain himself took a leading part in driving and keeping Gladstone from power, in favour of Lord Salisbury, for a period of nearly six years (1886–92). During the whole of this period, the rights and wrongs of the Conservatives' Irish policy formed the main basis of party contention but the Radical influence was at work in both camps.[1] The Gladstonians went to the country in 1892 on a much elaborated ver-

[1] See No. 68, however, for one characteristic aspect of working-class Radicalism, still capable of causing acute embarrassment at Westminster — the " Republican " readiness to decry the Jubilee celebrations of 1887.

sion of the *Radical Programme* adopted, in 1891, as the Newcastle Programme (No. 69), while Salisbury's Conservatives could claim to have given the country, with Chamberlain's aid, such valuable instalments of his original plan as the County Councils Act in 1888 and Free Education in 1891.

The scandals of Parnellism and anti-Parnellism, among their Irish Nationalist allies, deprived the Gladstonians of the commanding majority at which they had aimed when adopting the Newcastle Programme but, with the aid of both contending Irish factions, they succeeded in ejecting the Conservatives and taking office themselves for the period, 1892–5. Despite Irish preoccupations, the Gladstonians could claim to have given important benefits to the people, not merely in the Local Government Act of 1894, democratising local government and extending its social scope, but in the considerable administrative extensions which they had introduced, for example, into Factory and Mines Inspection and the increases of pay and reduction of hours which they had allowed in the Royal Dockyards and Arsenals.

Part of the attack, in fact, that finally developed against the " Radical " Government of 1892–5 and its Radical " Socialist " allies of the London County Council and the London School Board, turned on the dictation they were alleged to accept from a growing Trade Union movement whose restrictionist attitude towards production—" making the work go round " —was already felt by some to be the principal menace to the national economy.[1] Document 71

---

[1] No. 70 shows how Henry George himself had already taken a strong anti-Socialist stand. In Britain, Bradlaugh had done so too, not to mention Herbert Spencer.

illustrates other aspects which the political struggle of 1892–5 took—the Radical ambition, on the one hand, to introduce steeper taxation of large fortunes in order to offer the poor a " free breakfast table " (free, that is, of taxation), an ambition that found some partial satisfaction in the Harcourt Death Duties of 1894, and, on the other hand, the fierce Conservative counter-attack on the Radical " faddists and fanatics " whose shibboleths threatened to reduce the great British Empire to a very little England indeed.

The election of 1895, a disaster to the " party of progress ", gave power to a Conservative Government which, having annexed the former Liberal leader, Hartington, and the former Radical leader, Chamberlain, was hailed by its supporters as " the strongest Government of modern times ". In a period of mounting prosperity due, in large measure, to Imperialist expansion, the Radicals failed, for years, to work up a serious agitation against the Government (No. 72). The outbreak of the Boer War did not at first alter this, and Ministers, despite pro-Boer criticism from a strong Radical section, received another convincing majority at the General Election of 1900. Matters changed decisively, however, as the expensive war dragged on for nearly two years longer, and could not be terminated without burning down Boer farms and removing Boer women and children to concentration camps. There is already the note of anticipated triumph in Harcourt's very Radical treatment of Boer War costs in the Budget debate of April 1901 and in the Radical applause for Campbell-Bannerman's attacks on farm-burning and the concentration camps (No. 73).

Radical electoral chances were to increase steadily

as a result of nearly every political event of the next few years: the fierce and prolonged Dissenting opposition to the Education Act of 1902; the retirement of Lord Salisbury from the Prime Ministership; the complete inability of the new Prime Minister, Balfour, to keep Chamberlain from raising the controversial questions of Imperial Preference and Protection; and the gradual disintegration of the Conservative majority as dissension on Chamberlain's "Tariff Reform" grew worse. Even the succession of "bad winters" of post-war distress in the slums of the great cities had its importance, in promoting, among sections of the Opposition, a readiness to come to terms with Fabian Socialism (No. 74). The Radical case put to the country at the General Election of January 1906 is given in the form it took in the Election Address of Mr. Atherley-Jones, who had not only entered Parliament on the Radical wave of 1885 and sat continuously ever since but who, as the son of Ernest Jones, the Chartist leader, had an almost hereditary interest in the issue. The Address (No. 75) makes it obvious how much Radicalism had now been "socialised" and how far, too, Trade Union support had become a dominant electoral consideration if a Labour claim to a Radical seat were to be avoided.

The tendency to claim more and more for Labour grew steadily to 1914, and it was, perhaps, only the emergence of Lloyd George as the greatest platform success of the age that prevented relations between the Liberal Government and the Labour Party from degenerating into complete hostility. No. 76, quoting from Lloyd George's "Limehouse Speech" of 1909, shows the entertaining and rather vulgar electoral patter which Lloyd George developed for the working-class audience of the time. Up to 1914 he would probably have been counted as a greater platform asset than the whole Labour Party put together. But his war-time alliance with the Conservatives continued until the Conservative majority threw him over in 1922, ruined his reputation for political integrity both with the typical pre-war Radical (No. 77) and with the average working-class member of his pre-war audiences. The Labour Party was the great gainer and the inheritor of the Radical Tradition.

66: JOSEPH CHAMBERLAIN ON THE RADICAL PRO-
GRAMME: Speech at Warrington, September 8,
1885

WE have been looking to the extension of the franchise in order to bring into prominence questions which have been too long neglected. The great problem of our civilisation is unsolved. We have to account for and to grapple with the mass of misery and destitution in our midst, co-existent as it is with the evidence of abundant wealth ... It is a problem which some men would put aside by references to the eternal laws of supply and demand, to the necessity of freedom of contract, and to the sanctity of every private right of property. But, gentlemen, these phrases are the convenient cant of selfish wealth. They are no answers to our question. I quite understand the reason for timidity in dealing with this matter so long as Government was merely the expression of the will and prejudice of a limited few. Under such circumstances there might be good reason for not intrusting it with larger powers, even for the relief of this misery and destitution. But now that we have a Government of the people by the people, we will go on and make it the Government for the people, in which all shall co-operate in order to secure to every man his natural rights, his right to existence, and to a fair enjoyment of it. I shall be told to-morrow that this is Socialism. I have learnt not to be afraid of words that are flung in my face instead of argument. Of course it is Socialism. The Poor Law is Socialism; the Education Act is Socialism; the greater part of municipal work is Socialism; and every kindly act of legislation, by which the community has sought to discharge its responsibilities and obligations to the poor is Socialism; but it is none the worse for that. Our object is the elevation of the poor, of the masses of the people—a levelling up of them by which we shall do something to remove the excessive inequality in social life . . .

What is the Radical Programme? . . . The most important of these proposals refer to the question of the land . . . We propose to give the popular representative authorities the right to obtain land for all public purposes at its fair value, without paying an extortionate price to the landowner for the privilege of re-entering on what was the original possession of the whole community. We propose also that the local authority in every district, under proper conditions, shall have power to let land for labourers' allotments, for artisans' dwellings, and for small holdings. We do not suggest that they should part entirely with the property in, or the control of, the land. That should be reserved for the community alone. . . . I believe that in this way we could do something for the agricultural labourers, something also for the towns . . . Every working man in every town suffers by the competition of the cheap labour which comes in from the country . . .

There is another and a very important question . . .
schools . . . At the present time the total of fees
receivable in all the schools of England and Wales
amount to a little over a million and a half, and I believe
an addition to the income-tax of three farthings in the
pound, as one method of providing the money, would
be sufficient to throw open to-morrow every school-
house in the land. I claim the freedom of the schools
as a great aid to the spread of education, and as a just
concession to the necessities of the poor . . .

. . . Well, there are many other points in the Radical
programme . . . There is the question of the revision
of taxation. I think that taxation ought to involve
equality of sacrifice, and I do not see how this result is
to be obtained except by some form of graduated
taxation—that is, taxation which is proportionate to
the superfluities of the taxpayer. . . . Then there is the
question of the taxation of unoccupied land, of
sporting land, of ground rent, and of mineral royalties.
For my own part, I advocate all these methods of
taxation . . . Then there is the question of the Game
Laws. I cannot believe it possible that any Parliament
freely elected by the whole people will tolerate the
continuance of this anomalous—I would even say of
this barbarous—legislation . . . Lastly, there is the
proposal, the just demand, which has so much fluttered
some of our opponents, for an inquiry into the illegal
appropriation of public rights and public endowments;
and if this be found to have taken place within the
last half century, for their restitution, or for adequate
compensation . . .

(*Speeches of the Rt. Hon. Joseph Chamberlain*, ed. Henry
Lucy, 1885, pp. 188–190)

67: F. A. CHANNING: Speech at Kettering, July 1886

I SAID (at Kettering):— "Lord Randolph and Mr. Chamberlain had followed the fatal policy of severing Catholic and Protestant; Randolph preached civil war at Belfast, Chamberlain religious bigotry in Scotland and Wales.

"The Nationalist Movement had its faults, but at least led Catholic and Protestant to act together. Crime and outrage sprang from a horrible fever of revenge. Irish history was a long record of cruelties that made the blood run cold. In Queen Elizabeth's time, men, women, and children driven into pens for slaughter, little children hung by the roadside; in the great clearances families left starving on the hills. The guilt of Irish crime lies at our door—we have our share in the memories that have made Ireland disloyal. Our duty is to meet national sentiment, to do what we can to remove the causes of hatred.

"Home Rule had not been sprung on the country. In the Midlothian Manifesto of September (1885), they were asked to affirm the principle that the Irish people should manage their own affairs with protection for minorities . . . Mr. John Bright, who will always be regarded with love and affection . . . would deny the right of self-government because he cannot trust the men the Irish would elect. I ask whether the best man in the world, Mr. Gladstone himself or Mr. Bright, is entitled to choose representatives for people who should choose for themselves . . . Mr. Chamberlain in his heart feels he has made the great mistake of his life. The best way to reconcile all Liberals gone astray is to win a mighty victory in this election."

At Wollaston (I said): "All useful legislation was not being postponed for Irish questions; there had been grand work for the Scottish crofters; State regulation of vice had been swept away; Mr. Henry Richard by his motion had made it more difficult for a Government to engage in war without the consent of Parliament; the labour of children and young persons in shops had been lightened; more protection had been provided for miners in their work; while, by his (Mr. Channing's) own bill, a real start had been taken for the welfare of the railway servants. That Bill . . . and the County Government Bill which was ready for introduction . . . might have been passed, dealing with Local Government in Ireland too, providing allotments for labourers, the control of the liquor traffic, and other vital interests. Such a Bill, fairly before the country, would have prevented the foolish and wicked intriguing against Mr. Gladstone which went on in the lobbies for months past. That broad and wholesome programme had been arrested by the wanton rejection of Mr. Gladstone's Irish policy."

(*Memories of Midland Politics*, 1885–1910, by F. A. Channing, M.P. for East Northamptonshire, 1885–1910)

68: *The Queen's Jubilee. A Radical Protest issued by the Metropolitan Radical Federation*, 1887

QUEEN VICTORIA has been our sovereign for fifty years, and all the flunkeys of the country are preparing to celebrate her jubilee. All sorts of wild projects are mooted, and money is being raised by all sorts of means . . . It may safely be predicted that very little of the cash will be spent on useful objects . . . who will dare to say that any appreciable portion will go . . . to the relief of the honest struggling poor, whose lives are made more burdensome by the exactions of our monarchical system?

What are the flunkeys so pleased about? . . . Is there anything to be glad for except what we have achieved ourselves? Has Her Majesty done a millionth part as much for us as we have done for her?

The Queen has signed Acts of Parliament . . . She has borne an heir to the throne, and many other children . . . But there her credit account closes . . . Now let us look at Her Majesty's debit account. Since she came to the throne, we have paid her and her family the enormous sum of £23,220,000. Divided up, this comes to nearly £1,272 per day. Put in another way, it would support 5,936 families at 30s. per week.

Her Majesty derives additional income from large estates in England and Scotland, and moneys invested in other ways. She pays no income-tax, however . . . She owns all the immense property left by the late Prince Consort WHOSE WILL HAS NEVER BEEN PROVED . . . The Queen is a fabulously wealthy woman —how rich we may never know! Yet she gets the nation to support all her children, and to support them in the most extravagant fashion . . .

Pensions are also paid to the Queen's relatives . . . The grand total of these payments (to the Royal House) for 1884–5 was over £800,000. And this is exclusive of many thousand pounds spent on royal palaces and parks, and renovation and decoration of yachts, and royal trips. Altogether there is every reason why Royalty should celebrate the Jubilee . . . But why the people, who find all the money, should go wild with joy, is quite another question . . .

Fellow citizens, pause and reflect. Do not give way to the madness of the moment. Royalty is the head and fount of a foolish, wicked and costly system. You toil hard and your money is squandered in maintaining princes and princesses, aristocrats, state priests, swarms of useless officials and crowds of well-paid but inactive officers in the Army and Navy. Will you permit this for ever . . . ?

(This attack was directed against Queen Victoria's Jubilee celebrations.)

69: THE NEWCASTLE PROGRAMME, October 1891

MR. T. E. ELLIS moved a resolution declaring that the Disestablishment and Disendowment of the Church of England in Wales should be taken in the next Parliament as soon as Irish Home Rule was attained. This was seconded by Major Evans Jones, and carried unanimously. . . . Sir George Trevelyan moved and Mr. Storey seconded a motion on registration and electoral reform. This motion demanded . . . the appointment of responsible registration officers, the reduction of the qualifying period to three months, the abolition of the disqualifications now attaching to removals and one man one vote. The resolution further declared for shorter Parliaments, the placing on the rates of the expenses of Returning Officers at elections, the holding of all elections on one and the same day, and the recognition of the principle of the payment of members. Lord Ripon moved and Mr. R. W. Perks seconded a resolution declaring " that the condition of the rural population should receive the immediate attention of Parliament ". Three points were set forth as of primary importance. (A) The establishment of District and Parish Councils popularly elected. (B) The concessions of compulsory powers to local authorities to acquire and hold land for allotments, small holdings, village halls, places of worship, labourers' dwellings and other public purposes. (C) The reform of existing Allotment Acts by the removal of restrictions, by giving security of tenure, and the power to erect buildings and the right of full compensation for all improvements. . . . The last resolution was moved by Sir Wilfrid Lawson, again affirming the declarations of the Council in favour of "A thorough reform of the land laws, such as will secure—(a) the repeal of the laws of primogeniture and entail; (b) freedom of sale and transfer; (c) the just taxation of land values and ground rents; (d) compensation to town and country tenants, for both disturbance and improvement, together with a simplified process for obtaining such compensation; (e) The enfranchisement of leaseholds.

"The direct popular veto on the liquor traffic;

"The Disestablishment and Disendowment of the Established Church in Scotland;

"The equalization of the Death Duties upon real and personal property;

"The just division of rates between owner and occupier;

"The taxation of Mining Royalties;

"A 'Free Breakfast Table';

"The extension of the Factory Acts; and

"The 'mending or ending' of the House of Lords."

(The Radical Programme adopted by the National Liberal Federation at its Newcastle Conference in 1891. (P. W. Clayden's *England under the Coalition* (1892), pp. 538–542))

70: HENRY GEORGE: *The Condition of Labour,* 1891

WHAT the Socialists seek is the assumption by the State of capital . . . or more properly speaking of large capitals, and State management and direction of at least the larger operations of industry. In this way they hope to abolish interest, which they regard as a wrong and an evil; to do away with the gains of exchangers, speculators, contractors, and middlemen, which they regard as waste; to do away with the wage-system and secure general co-operation; and to prevent competition, which they deem the fundamental cause of the impoverishment of labour. . . .

With the Socialists we have some points of agreement, for we recognize fully the social nature of man and believe that all monopolies should be held and governed by the State. In these, and in directions where the general health, knowledge, comfort, and convenience might be improved, we, too, would extend the functions of the State.

But it seems to us the vice of Socialism in all its degrees is its want of radicalism, of going to the root . . . It assumes that the tendency of wages to a minimum is the natural law, and seeks to abolish wages; it assumes that the natural result of competition is to grind down workers, and seeks to abolish competition by restrictions, prohibitions, and extensions of governing power . . . It fails to see that what it mistakes for the evils of competition are really the evils of restricted competition—are due to a one-sided competition to which men are forced when deprived of land. While its methods, the organisation of men into industrial armies, the direction and control of all production and exchange by governmental or semigovernmental bureaux, would, if carried to full expression mean Egyptian despotism.

We differ from the Socialists in our diagnosis of the evil, and we differ from them as to remedies. We have no fear of capital, regarding it as the natural hand-maiden of labour; we look on interest in itself as natural and just; we would set no limit to accumulation, nor impose on the rich any burden that is not equally placed on the poor; we see no evil in competition, but deem unrestricted competition to be as necessary to the health of the industrial and social organism as the free circulation of the blood is to the health of the bodily organism—to be the agency whereby the fullest co-operation is to be secured. We would simply take for the community what belongs to the community, the value that attaches to land by the growth of the community . . .

71A: The *Northern Echo,* January 15, 1894

A MEMORIAL signed by nearly one hundred Radical members has been presented to Sir William Harcourt, praying him to make his Budget one of drastic financial reform by graduating the income tax, and increasing and graduating the duties on personal property passing at death, and equalising those duties on personal and real property. If these suggestions are adopted, the memorialists contend that the Chancellor of the Exchequer will be able to make tea, coffee, cocoa, and dried fruits duty free, to provide funds for making the Government a model employer of labour both as regards hours and wages, to pay members of Parliament and the cost of elections, to extend national education and improve the position of the aged and deserving poor, to provide for the deficit in the national finances and for any expenditure necessary to strengthen the navy . . .

71B: E. ASHMEAD-BARTLETT, M.P.: Article in the *North American Review*, June 1894

THE writer denounces the "heterogeneous mass of faddists, crocheteers, fanatics, Home Rulers, and revolutionaries that compose the Radical party . . . (made up) of Irish Nationalists, of Disestablishmentarians, both Welsh and Scotch, of Registration Reformers of many varieties, of Trades Unionists, of Socialists and of Teetotallers, not to say anything about anti-vaccinators, anti-vivisectionists, anti-opium men, and the advocates of peace at any price . . . The Separatist and Radical fads and prejudices of Irishmen, Scotchmen and Welshmen are humoured and favoured in every possible way. . . . A whole English county, Monmouthshire, which has never been in Wales, and which is entirely English in language and preponderatingly English in blood, is to be filched from England and deprived of its church, in order to gratify Welsh Disestablishers. The Scotch are to have a separate Scotch Grand Committee for Scotch Affairs . . . Ireland and Wales are to have similar separate Grand Committees. There is to be no separate Grand Committee for England. English affairs and English interests are still to be dominated and controlled in Parliament by Scotch and Welsh and Irish Radicals . . . The Irish Nationalists have twenty-three seats more in Parliament than they are entitled to . . . The Welsh Radicals have three more seats . . .

72: F. A. CHANNING: *Memories of Midland Politics*
1892

I BEAR a mandate which cannot be misunderstood, the message of your hearts to cheer our great leader. Ireland is no longer under Mr. Balfour, and England is no longer under Lord Salisbury. England with its parish councils, free land for the people, schools under popular control, new labour laws—England is passing into a new era . . .

The majority might be small, but Mr. Gladstone had behind him men who had passed through the fire. Between the stages of Home Rule they could deal with Bills for Registration, Plural Voting, Parish Councils, power to buy land at its fair value—the whole programme of making the world better for the workers . . .

Mr. Gladstone could have formed two or three Ministries out of materials available. The Ministry might have been stronger, more effective for their purposes, if more democratic. But they commanded confidence, and would do their best to pass sound Radical measures . . . Registration, one man one vote, all elections on one day, and as cheap as local elections; shorter Parliaments, democratic parish councils with real power as to land and charities, control of schools, cheap land transfer, bold tenure and labour reforms, and local option—a big programme, but they were resolved to have it from this Ministry.

1895

Their hearts were true to the principles which had won three mighty victories in that Division . . . Ten years before he came before them as a convinced Radical. Ten years of the House of Commons, fighting the stubborn obstruction of privilege, had made him ten times more Radical than ever. Liberals had tried to carry out every pledge. Conservatives had obstructed every generous proposal, reversed every cherished hope, sown dissension in the forces which worked for the aspirations of the future. What had been going on at Derby, Bradford, and elsewhere was the Devil's work. The country would not surrender to the Tory Party. The people would resent this plot to destroy the future of democracy by putting them under the heels of peers and brewers, under the dictation of the priesthood. If they thought he had lived up to their and his own ideal, he hoped they would add one more vote and voice to the cause of Progress in the House of Commons.

1899

If some of the democracy had not let themselves be bamboozled about Mr. Gladstone's democratic solution for Irish troubles into handing back power twice to the Tories, this country would have had a chapter of reform such as they could scarcely dream of.

That was the spirit in which democracy had been played with for fifteen years. He was there as a democrat. Were they satisfied with the policy which had brought war and trouble, with these repeated betrayals of the interest of the people? Why not revert to the creed of treating others as they would be treated themselves . . . ?

What did Imperialism mean for democracy? Imperialism ministered to class interests. Class rapacity abroad meant class rapacity at home.

Imperialism meant overwhelming taxation, which the poor paid in higher proportion than the rich, and they would want more and more men, till conscription ended their liberties. These were the perils of limitless growth of Militarism.

1900

In bye-elections up to July 1899, the country had gone against the Tories twice as fast as it ever went against. Mr. Gladstone. They wanted to shut out social reforms just as they would inquiry into the mismanagement which landed the country in war and peril and disaster, and led on to the ghastly fever-tents at Bloemfontein. They hurried the election before the war was over, and before the truth was known. They were sheltering themselves behind Lord Roberts and Sir George White and Baden-Powell. They were asking a " Khaki Vote ". I was fighting because this was a fight of democracy against the greatest curse of the age, financial Imperialism! This South African War meant the churning up of the whole world to make butter for the rich. The war, say what Mr. Chamberlain might, was the direct outcome of the capitalists' conspiracy to seize the mines. The Transvaal Government blocked the way of schemes to lower wages of English miners, and employ Kaffirs and Chinese at a tenth of what they paid under Kruger. The war was unjust. Mr. Chamberlain's policy had provoked the Transvaal to invade Natal as an act of self-defence . . .

I asked their votes in the interests of labour and of humane and just treatment of weaker races, whom they should not crush and enslave, but enlist as friends . . .

(Channing here gives a picture of the constituency of East Northants which he represented as a Radical from 1885 to 1910. (*Memories of Midland Politics* by F. A. Channing, 1918))

73A: SIR WILLIAM HARCOURT: Speech in the House of
Commons, April 18, 1901

UP to the present time the cost of this war has been
£148,000,000, and what it will be before it is over, the
rt. hon. gentleman does not even conjecture . . . We
have new doctrines upon the subject of taxation . . . as
I read this newspaper finance, it seems to me that the
fashionable doctrine of to-day may be condensed into
two words—conscription and protection . . . Does any
one believe that this expenditure and this borrowing is
not going to be increased? Has any one read the
dispatch of Sir Alfred Milner? . . . He tells you that
the last six months of the war have been retrogressive
in South Africa and that the condition of things is
much worse . . . than six months ago . . . We have a
scheme propounded for this settlement in South Africa
when the war is over. The object of that settlement is
fairly stated. It is to establish in South Africa a British
garrison and a British electorate . . . What is the scheme
going to cost? . . . I venture to think that the country
is beginning already to ask what it is to profit by this
war. It has got up to this time taxation and debt and
future liability which I think will cost you as much as
the war has cost. What have you gained besides? You
have gained the paralysis of all reform at home [Hear,
hear]. There is the question of the housing of the poor.
What has become of that? In connexion with old age
pensions and education, what might have been done
with that £140,000,000. It is all gone . . . There is this
curious thing, which I have always observed in
Imperialists—namely that they have a great regard for
the British Empire generally, but there is one part of

215

the British Empire which they always forget, and that is the United Kingdom of 40 millions of people [Cheers] ... these 40 millions will one day require some regard to be paid to their interests ...

(*The Times*, April 19, 1901)

73B: SIR H. CAMPBELL-BANNERMAN: Speech at Peckham, August 7, 1901

WE can see the blunders and miscalculations of the politicians who have controlled events [Cheers]. They were surprised when they found that the Boers intended to fight. They were surprised when they found that they could ride [Laughter and cheers]. They were surprised when they found that they could shoot [Laughter]. They were surprised when they found that their brethren of the Orange Free State were going to join them [A cry of "Good luck to them" and cheers] ... And month by month they have been wrong in their estimate of the duration of the war ... [Loud and continued groans for Chamberlain] ... I have denounced and, Heaven helping me, will continue to denounce [Loud cheers] all this stupid policy of farm-burning [Cries of "Shame"], devastation, and the sweeping of women and children into camps [Renewed cries of "Shame"] ... Now we have the Colonial Secretary speaking to us of leniency being regrettable. He says that strong measures will be taken in certain cases ... And another thing that is threatened is that the Kaffirs should be used and armed ... Therefore a new question arises now. It is no longer a question whether the war was just or unjust, it is a question whether it should be prosecuted at all hazards and by all means. This would mean the extermination of the people against whom we are fighting. I ask you have the British people for a moment given their sanction to this?

(*The Times*, August 8, 1901)

74: L. CHIOZZA MONEY: *Riches and Poverty*, 1905

AT present the greater part of the labours of social reformers are directed to dealing with a succession of distressful effects. Here are slums; how shall we re-house their inmates? Here are paupers; what shall we do with them? Here are unemployed; how shall we keep them going until they find employers? Here are aged poor; can we, should we, give them pensions? We owe a present duty in all these and many other matters . . . But ever we must keep before us the causes which bring into being the raw material of our social problems; ever we must have clear vision of the crime of poverty in a wealthy country; ever we must seek to come to grips with the original sin.

To deal with causes we must strike at the Error of Distribution by gradually substituting public ownership for private ownership of the means of production. In no other way can we secure for each worker in the hive the full reward of his labour. So long as between the worker and his just wage stands the private landlord and the private capitalist, so long will poverty remain, and not poverty alone, but the moral degradations which inevitably arise from the devotion of labour to the service of waste. So long as the masses of the people are denied the fruit of their own labour so long will our civilisation be a false veneer, and our every noble thoroughfare be flanked by purlieus of shame.

There is already a beginning made. A few hundred millions have been applied as public capital in the ownership by many municipalities of such services as tramways, gasworks, and waterworks ... Such capital is yet but a tiny fraction of the whole, and it still bears a great mortgage and pays interest to private hands. That interest, in process of time, will disappear through the operation of sinking funds, and then, as to certain services, the community will enter into its own with no tribute to pay to private usurers. From the small beginnings made we must seek to advance ...

... The greater number of our industrial concerns are already shaped in the form of limited liability companies, the shareholders in which are dumb, while the management is in the hands of paid officials. The reform which needs to be effected is to substitute the community at large for the dumb shareholders. Management ability, invention would be properly rewarded ... The only change would be the gradual substitution of the community for the shareholders, and the consequent disappearance of unearned incomes. Such portions of the product as were necessary for application as new capital would be so applied by the community. For the rest, the whole of the product would go to labour. Saving, the necessary saving, without which labour would go without tools, would be simply and automatically effected, and capital would take its true and rightful place as the handmaiden of labour.

... The organizer, the man of arrangement, will be invited to exercise his talent, not in over-reaching and despoiling his fellows, but in planning their welfare in a thousand new schemes of development ... Accounts will be simple and clerks few. No travellers, agents or touts will be needed to push doubtful commodities. The sham and the substitute will be found only in museums.

(L. Chiozza Money's *Riches and Poverty*; First edition 1905; Fifth Edition 1908. Sir Leo Chiozza Money was a Radical M.P. from 1906 to 1918, when he joined the Labour Party, apparently the first Liberal Front-Bencher to do so.)

75: L. A. ATHERLEY-JONES: Election Address, January 1906 (Atherley-Jones was a Radical M.P. from 1885 to 1914)

To the Electors of North-West Durham.

Gentlemen,—To the great satisfaction of the Country, the Tory Government has come to an ignominious end; it has taken the extraordinary course of resigning while it still possessed a Parliamentary majority . . .

Since 1895 it has enjoyed, with a huge Parliamentary majority, every opportunity of legislating; all that it could perform in 10 years for the good of the people was to pass the Workmen's Compensation Act, in many respects an inadequate and unsatisfactory measure.

But it has been active in looking after the interests of the Church, the Liquor Trade and the Landowner; it has passed an Education Act which has compelled Nonconformists to pay for the support of Schools managed by the Clergy and exclusively controlled by Teachers belonging to the Established Church; it has afforded to the owners of public-house property a State guarantee . . . ; it has relieved Agricultural Land of a large share of the rates which means not relief to the Farmer and Labourer, but a larger rent for the Landowner and heavier taxation for the Inhabitants of Towns . . .

Their evil work does not end here; they have increased the National Debt and raised taxation to an amount never before reached . . . The wealthy they spared, but imposed their taxation on the poor. They even taxed Corn and Flour, and, when forced to abandon this, imposed a Tax on Coal which British miners have to pay.

They have violated the noblest traditions of the Country by re-establishing slavery under the British flag at the bidding of a few Foreign Capitalists.

Now at length the Liberal party is in power. The task before them is indeed heavy . . .

The first duty of the Government, as declared by the Prime Minister, will be to establish Religious Equality in our Educational system and to combine public expenditure with public control . . .

We shall not delay . . . in repealing the Coal Tax . . .

Protection to the Funds of Trade Unions, recognition of the full right of combination by workmen, a righteous and thorough reform of our land laws in which alone security for the health and prosperity of our population is to be found, larger powers to our municipalities for providing decent dwellings for the people, a reform of the licensing laws in conformity with the demands of public opinion and co-operation between the State and our great friendly societies . . . in providing for the aged and infirm, reform of our electoral laws on the basis of a franchise that recognises no distinction of wealth or sex. These and others are the projects to which Liberal activity should be directed . . .

Protection means perhaps that a few rich people will be made richer, but it certainly means that the many poor will be made poorer . . .

I have served you for Twenty years in Parliament. If you think I have been diligent, honest and upright . . . will you give me the reward I crave, that I may continue to be your loyal and devoted representative in Parliament . . .

76: ·D. LLOYD GEORGE: Speech at Limehouse, July 30, 1909

. . . I HAVE just one other land tax, and that is a tax on royalties. The landlords are receiving eight millions a year by way of royalties. What for? They never deposited the coal there [Laughter]. It was not they who planted the great granite rocks in Wales, who laid the foundations of the mountains. Was it the landlord? [Laughter]. And yet he, by some divine right, demands as his toll—for merely the right of our men to risk their lives in hewing these rocks—eight millions a year! Take any coalfield. I went down to a coalfield the other day, and they pointed out to me many collieries there. They said: "You see that colliery there. The first man who went there spent a quarter of a million in sinking shafts, in driving mains and levels. He never got coal, and he lost his quarter of a million. The second man who came spent £100,000—and he failed. The third man came along, and he got the coal." What was the landlord doing in the meantime? The first man failed; but the landlord got his royalty. . . . The second man failed, but the landlord got his royalty.

These capitalists put their money in, and I said, "When the cash failed, what did the landlord put in?" He simply put in the bailiffs [Loud laughter]. The capitalist risks, at any rate, the whole of his money; the engineer puts his brain in: the miner risks his life ... In the very next colliery to the one I descended, just a few years ago, 300 people lost their lives ... and yet when the Prime Minister and I knock at the door of these great landlords, and say to them: "Here, you know these poor fellows who have been digging up royalties at the risk of their lives, some of them are old, they have survived the perils of their trade, they are broken, they can earn no more. Won't you give something to keep them out of the workhouse?" they scowl at you, and we say, "Only a ha'penny, just a copper." They say, "You thieves!" And they turn their dogs on to us, and you can hear their bark every morning [Loud laughter and cheers]. If this is an indication of the view taken by these great landlords of their responsibility to the people who, at the risk of life, create their wealth, then I say their day of reckoning is at hand [Loud cheers] ...

I claim that the tax we impose on land is fair, is just, and is moderate [Cheers]. They go on threatening that if we proceed they will cut down their benefactions and discharge labour. What is the labour they are going to choose for dismissal? Are they going to threaten to devastate rural England by feeding and dressing themselves? Are they going to reduce their gamekeepers? Ah, that would be sad! [Laughter] ... But what would happen to you in the season? No week-end shooting with the Duke of Norfolk or anyone [Laughter]. But that is not the kind of labour they are going to cut down. They are going to cut down the

productive labour—their builders and their gardeners
. . . and they are going to ruin their property so that
it shall not be taxed. All I can say is this: the ownership of land is not merely an enjoyment, it is a
stewardship [Cheers]. It has been reckoned as such in
the past, and if they cease to discharge their functions,
the security and defence of the country, looking after
the broken in their villages and in their neighbourhoods
—then those functions, which are part of their tradi-
tional duties . . . if they cease to discharge those
functions, the time will come to reconsider the
conditions under which land is held in this country
[Loud cheers]. No country, however rich, can
permanently afford to have quartered upon its revenue
a class which declines to do the duty which it was called
upon to perform since the beginning [Hear, hear].

77: D. LLOYD GEORGE: Speech of July 1, 1913

AT the back of the Tory mind you find this: Tories
firmly believe that Providence has singled them out to
govern this land. They think that they are the
governing classes, and that if they are not governing
there must be something wrong. In 1906 they were
turned out of power. They thought it was just a
temporary visitation . . . But when a second election
came with the same result and a third election came
and Radicals were still in power, the Tories became
troubled. They saw Radical Bills go through Parliament, and, what was still worse, they found Tories
expected to obey them as if they were common people.
They found Radicals on the Benches as Magistrates
and Radicals becoming Judges. They found Radicals
as Ministers receiving Kings and Presidents. They saw

Radicalism governing the Empire, and things were getting from bad to worse. And they said, " There is no knowing that it might not even happen again. There is the Plural Voting Bill." They found trade prospering and the country going on, and at last their balance is completely upset . . . Supposing I had devoted as much time and energy to defending privilege and monopoly in land, in the Church Establishment, in the liquor traffic, in the House of Lords, as I have devoted to assailing them, do you think a word would have been said in the Tory Press . . . in regard to this (" Marconi Scandal ") matter? No, what has happened to us has happened because in office we have stood by the people who put us there.

> (H. Duparcq, *David Lloyd George*, Vol. IV, p. 818. In this speech, Lloyd George gave his own explanation of why he had been attacked in the " Marconi Scandal ".)

78: R. B. HALDANE: *An Autobiography*

IN 1918 the Liberal party went to pieces, and I had to consider whether it was desirable to try to work with it again in the condition into which it had then fallen . . . There was a growing Labour organisation to be taken into account. Labour was gaining seats rapidly. Its support came less from its official leaders than from men and women who had before them an ideal with which I was definitely in sympathy, that of equality of chance in life. What seemed wisest was accordingly to continue rather aloof from Liberal organisations and to get such a contact with Labour as would enable me to understand it. I began to speak at Labour meetings and to see a good deal of Labour members . . . In the end of 1923 . . . Ramsay Macdonald . . . wrote to me to know whether I would try to assist him in forming a Government . . . I wrote an affectionate letter to Asquith, explaining how I found myself compelled to join my fortunes with Labour . . . I wished to resume the Lord Chancellorship and to lead the party in the Lords . . . After a prolonged talk at Cloan, Macdonald expressed his concurrence . . . and on these terms I became Lord Chancellor in his Government . . . Particularly in the early days of 1924 I was of use in a special way to my colleagues for I had had experience of the nuances of the Constitution, and of the proper course to be taken by Ministers, in theory servants of the Crown as well as its advisers . . .

(Richard Burdon Haldane. An *Autobiography*, 1929, p. 307 et sqq. Lord Haldane, before the War a Liberal Minister, became Lord Chancellor after the War in the first Labour Government.)

APPENDIX

THOUGH modern English Radicalism has been treated as having originated in the eighteenth century, it is true that sixteenth and seventeenth century Puritan Parliamentarians tended to take, in their quarrels with the Crown and its ministers, attitudes surprisingly parallel. It would be difficult to trace any line of connection between Peter Wentworth and Pym, on the one hand, and Wilkes and Paine on the other. But there would seem to have been some study, by the more modern "reformers", of Parliamentary Puritan models before the characteristic style of the Radical Petition was developed. One of the most characteristic Petitions of the Long Parliament to Charles I is printed below so that it may be compared with the petitioning styles of the eighteenth and nineteenth century Radicals.

To the King's Most Excellent Majesty

The humble Petition of the Lords and Commons, now assembled in Parliament.

We Your Majesty's most loyal subjects, the Lords and Commons in Parliament, cannot without great grief . . . behold the pressing miseries, the imminent danger, and the devouring calamities, which do extremely threaten, and have partly seized upon both your Kingdoms of England and Ireland, by the practices of a party prevailing with your Majesty; who by many wicked plots and conspiracies have attempted the alteration of the true religion, and of the ancient government of this kingdom, by the introducing of Popish superstition and idolatry into the Church, and tyranny and confusion in the State, and, for the compassing thereof,

227

have long corrupted your Majesty's counsels, abused your
power, and, by sudden and untimely dissolving of former
Parliaments, have often hindered the reformation, and prevention of those mischiefs; who, being now disabled to avoid
the endeavours of this Parliament by any such means, have
traiterously attempted to overawe the same by force, and in
prosecution of their wicked designs, have excited, encouraged,
and fostered an unnatural rebellion in Ireland, by which in a
cruel and most outrageous manner, many of your subjects
there have been destroyed; and by false slanders upon your
Parliament, and by malicious and unjust accusations, they
have endeavoured to begin the like massacre here, but, being
disappointed therein by the blessing of God, they have (as
the most mischievous and bloody design of all) won upon
your Majesty to make war against your Parliament and good
subjects of this Kingdom, leading in your own person an
army against them, as if you intended by conquest to establish
an absolute and unlimited power over them . . . : And, for
their better assistance in these wicked designs, do seek to bring
over the rebels of Ireland, and other forces from beyond the
seas to join with them: And we finding ourselves utterly
deprived of your Majesty's protection, and the authors,
counsellors, and abettors of these mischiefs in greatest power
and favour with your Majesty, and defended by you against
the justice and authority of Your High Court of Parliament
. . . we have for the just and necessary defence of the Protestant Religion, of your Majesty's person, Crown and dignity, of
the laws and liberties of the Kingdom, and the power and
privilege of Parliament, taken up arms, and appointed and
authorised Robert Earl of Essex to be Captain General . . .
and them to subdue and bring to condign punishment; and
we do most humbly beseech your Majesty to withdraw your
royal presence and countenance from these wicked persons . . .
but in peace and safety (without your forces) forthwith return
to your Parliament, and by your faithful counsel and advice
compose the present distempers . . . wherein if your Majesty

please to yield to our most humble and earnest desires, we do, in the presence of Almighty God, profess that we will receive your Majesty with all honour, yield you all due obedience and subjection, and faithfully endeavour to secure your person and estate from all danger. . . .

(Harleian Miscellany, i, 218–219)

INDEX